How Great a Love

How Great a Love

Faith, Forgiveness, and the Father

KYLE A. SMITH

RESOURCE *Publications* · Eugene, Oregon

Resource Publications
An Imprint of Wipf and Stock Publishers
199 W. 8th Ave., Suite 3
Eugene, OR 97401

www.wipfandstock.com

PAPERBACK ISBN: 978-1-6667-1592-7
HARDCOVER ISBN: 978-1-6667-1593-4
EBOOK ISBN: 978-1-6667-1594-1

AUGUST 10, 2021

This book is dedicated to my mom and stepdad,
dad and stepmom, grandma, the rest of my family,
and to those who thought it was worthwhile to share
the love of Jesus with me.

"As the Father has loved me, so have I loved you. Abide in my love."

JOHN 15:9

Contents

Acknowledgments | ix

Preface | xi

1   Dad | 1

2   Mine | 9

3   Waiting and Watching | 19

4   Hide and Seek | 28

5   Enter the Throne Room | 38

6   The Man at the Well | 50

7   There Was Jesus | 60

8   The Battle | 71

9   A Change of Clothing | 82

10   The Other Kyle Smith | 92

Afterword | 102

Bibliography | 105

Acknowledgments

Thank you, Jess. Without you, this book would have never come to fruition. I love you. My gratitude also goes out to all of those who have encouraged me in my faith and my writing. I will be forever thankful for your support.

Preface

I SAT THERE ACROSS from the therapist and was explaining how my life had fallen apart. He had me take a test to check my mental state. Upon reviewing my answers, he told me that I was severely depressed. I had no disagreements with that assessment. I had always been a happy-go-lucky person that meandered through life with a constant smile. All of my joy seemed to have been drained from me. I knew that I was a shell of myself. Worst of all, for the first time in my life, I felt as though I was not loved.

Over the following year, God reminded me again and again that his love for me—for all of us— never dissipates based on life's circumstances. He not only brought me through the darkest time in my life, but he also revealed to me an aspect of himself that I had overlooked for far too long: he is our loving father. My faith became renewed, and I felt his affection in ways that I had never experienced before. My hope for this book is that you will come to know that you are God's child, and you are loved beyond anything that you can ever imagine.

1

Dad

THERE ARE MANY WAYS in which someone can view God: king, creator, giver, warrior, judge, etc. The way that I most often view God is the way that Jesus introduced to us, father. Father is a loaded word. For some people, it elicits positive feelings. You think of the love, warmth, joy, and fun that your father provided. Your mind drifts off to family vacations, holiday traditions, going to sporting events, and the myriad of other memories that brings a smile to your face. For others, unfortunately, it may conjure up the negative emotions of disappointment, abandonment, hurt, or shame. Sometimes fathers are not who they should be and leave a wake of pain in their path. I am one of the lucky ones. I have a great and loving relationship with my father. That may be the foundation of why I view God the way that I do. Throughout this book, I am going to share stories from both the Bible and my life that speak to God as our father.

The concept of God as father was not a new concept in Jesus' day. In fact, there are several passages in the Old Testament that allude to viewing God in this way. You can look to Jeremiah 31:9, where God says, "For I am a father to Israel." Malachi 2:10 speaks to this as well, "Have we not all one father? Has not one

1

God created us?" There are a few more passages, but this way of viewing God was not widely prominent before Jesus' incarnation.

This changed when Jesus took on flesh and began his earthly ministry. We first see this in Luke 2, when Jesus was twelve years old. His family had gone to Jerusalem for the Passover feast. The feast was finished, and they were heading back home to Nazareth. It would have taken them about a week to make the trip. After the first day, Mary and Joseph looked around for little-boy Jesus, but he wasn't there. Let's cut his parents some slack here. They were traveling with a large group of friends and family and assumed he was in the group. After all, they would have made this journey many times. After frantically searching among the travel party, they realized that Jesus was nowhere to be found.

Panic set in. I think any parent can imagine the emotions that would come along with not knowing where your child is. Now, imagine that you've lost God's son. Mary and Joseph must have been heartbroken and scared beyond comprehension, wondering what had happened to their son. Finally, they decided to check the Temple. This would have probably been the last place where they saw him. Lo and behold, there sat Jesus, not yet a man, amongst the religious teachers, amazing them with his words. It took them three days to find Jesus. This wouldn't be the last time that Mary lost her son for three days.

Mary was hurt when she found her son. Scripture doesn't say, but I believe we can surmise the thoughts that were going through her mind. It was probably something like, "We have been searching all over for you! We didn't know what had happened to you. We didn't know if you were dead or alive. Here you are, just sitting here as if nothing is wrong!" Those may have been her thoughts, but what she asked was, "Son, why have you treated us so?" Then Jesus said these astonishing words, "Why were you looking for me? Did you not know that I must be in my father's house?"

The word 'my' is a gamechanger in that statement. The first recorded public event of Jesus' life was him referring to God not only as the Father but as "my father." This was beyond the Jewish understanding of who God was. When they referred to God as father, it was much more as creator, which was the chief way that they viewed God. When Jesus referred to God as father, he was suggesting intimacy. This is not a reference to a God who is a million miles away. No, this is talking about an up-close, personal God. The concept of who God is was much different for Jesus than those with whom he was sitting.

Jesus takes this concept of God even further throughout his ministry. He explains to us over and over again that God is our father as well. This is most prominent in the book of Matthew. Eighteen different times, Jesus said either "your father" or "our father." This is a big deal. With these words, Jesus is informing us that we are invited into that same, intimate relationship with the Father that he has. He is telling us to shift our image of God from the white-bearded deity in the sky to one who deeply cares for and loves us. This was a radical and revolutionary statement in ancient Israel because that's not how they viewed God. Sadly, it is still a radical and revolutionary statement today.

How we view God has not changed much over the past few thousand years. The Jews viewed God as one who would bless them if they did well and punish them if they failed. This is seen in the encounter in John 9. Jesus and his disciples were walking down the road when they saw a man who was born blind. One of the disciples asked Jesus, "Rabbi, who sinned, this man or his parents, that he was born blind?" That was the prevailing mindset at the time. Because this man had a disability, God must have been punishing either him or his parents. (Much, much more on John 9 to come in chapter 7 of this book.) God was the eternal judge, holding the cosmic scales of right and wrong in his hands. As long as you were doing well, your life would go well. The minute that you faltered, God was out to get you. The thing that this god most cared about was people following the rules. There were hundreds and hundreds of rules, most of which were man-made.

We have yet to shake that image of God. This is the basis for the heretical prosperity gospel that is very prevalent in our world today. You are promised health and wealth as long as you uphold your end of the deal. This god operates much like interest on your savings account. The more you put in, the more you will get. But rest assured, the prosperity gospel preachers haven't cornered the market on this notion of God. On the other end, there are the legalists. Really though, they're two sides of the same coin. Legalists see God as the almighty judge who is ready to strike down all the heathens who can't follow the rules. They believe that the most important aspect of the relationship that you can have with God is to fear him. Not fear in the biblical sense which means to revere and be in awe of God. This fear is synonymous with going to the principal's office after getting in trouble at school. God exists to keep you in line. If you get out of line, then he's going to drop the hammer on you. The only sort of love that is involved here is tough love. Both of these postulations of the character of God are travesties. They do not line up with the God that we see in the Bible. They create a god who wants more and more from us, whether that be to give more or to be more. With this being the only god that many hear about, it's no wonder why so many have left the faith or have no interest in it. There can be no real relationship with these gods. We will work ourselves to death trying to please them and always coming up short. These polluted images of God do not suggest, as Jesus does, that he is a loving father.

In the first of his three letters, John had this to say at the beginning of chapter 3 (via the Holman Christian Standard Bible), "Look at how great a love the Father has given us that we should be called God's children. And we are!" You will be hard-pressed to find a more beautifully written verse in scripture. We are God's children, and he is our father. How amazing is that! The Bible does not speak about a distant god, but a god who is near to us. The same God who created all that there is in this world and beyond, who put the stars in their place, and set our solar system to revolve around the sun, is the God who most desires to be in a deep, meaningful relationship with you. Why? Because we are his children, and he is a perfect and loving father. That is all that there is to it. It doesn't make sense to us. We will never understand why perfection is so infatuated with imperfection. We will never understand why God "so loved the world" when much of the world is hard to love (John 3:16). We will never understand why God chooses us to be his children while we often choose other gods. These are the mysteries of faith, but it is who he is.

I don't know about you, but I don't think, when talking to him, that I have ever called my earthly father "father." I have always called him dad. Father just sounds too formal to me. Dad suggests a closer relationship. In fact, the first word that most children learn is "dada." Brennan Manning, who you will hear from throughout this book, explains it like this in The Furious Longing of God:

> American child psychologists tell us that the average American baby begins to speak between the ages of four-teen and eighteen months. Regardless of the sex of the child, the first word normally spoken at that age is *da*—da, da, daddy. A little Jewish child speaking Aramaic in first-century Palestine at the same age level would begin to say *ab*—ab, ab, Abba . . . Jesus is saying that we may address the infinite, transcendent, almighty God with intimacy, familiarity, and unshaken trust that a sixteen-month-old baby has sitting on his father's lap – *da, da, daddy*.[1]

God is not just our father, but he is our Abba. He is our dad. Our relationship is not built on formality and unfamiliarity. No, it is built on closeness. This is how God differs from all other dei-ties throughout all other religions. Every single other god that has been created since the beginning of time is an impersonal god who stays separated from the people. The relationship between false gods and devotees is simple, work to achieve approval.

Sadly, this is a common trait amongst earthly fathers as well. I have been involved with sports all of my life, namely football. I have been both a player and a coach. Far too often, I would see dads only tell their children that they were proud of them if they played well. I have seen the heartbreak of many when, after a loss, they would look to their father for support and encouragement only to find a more crushing defeat awaiting them. This happens outside of the sporting realm as well. Too many times are love and

---

1. Manning, *The Furious Longing of God*, 43–44.

approval only expressed to a kid when they have achieved something or have become exactly who their father wanted them to be. Plenty of adults suffer from an inferiority complex because their dads were never satisfied with them. They were never enough, and now, they believe that is who they are.

"Look at how great a love the Father has given us that we should be called God's children. And we are!" How's that for a juxtaposition? Our perfect and loving father has told us that he is satisfied with us, that he does love us, and that he accepts us for who we are. It's not about working to please him. It's about accepting that we are his and that he will always be there for us, even when we fail. Romans 5:8 explains how much we mean to our heavenly father, "But God shows his love for us in that while we were still sinners, Christ died for us." He not only tells us that he loves us, but he also proved it by sending his son to die for us. God didn't wait until we got everything right. He didn't say, "If you achieve, then I will love you." He didn't lay out the five things that you have to do to become his child. He saw us in our lowly, sinful state and did everything he could to bring us to him. It doesn't matter if you score the game-winning touchdown or your team loses by one hundred, you are accepted and loved. That is all there is to it. Yes, it seems farcical in its simplicity, but that is how absurdly your Abba loves you.

In 2016, during Chris Tomlin's Worship Night in America, Max Lucado, a pastor and author, told this story. He was visiting Jerusalem, and he heard the voice of a small girl crying out in the crowded street, "Abba! Abba!" It was obvious that the little girl had gotten separated from her father and was lost. Lucado decided to stand back and watch what happened. As the scared girl kept crying for her dad, he noticed a man that began to frantically make his way back to the child. This was a busy street, and he had to fight his way to her. Finally, the father reached his child. He scooped her up in his arms and held her tightly. He knew that she must have been afraid that she would never see her dad again. He then put her down and told her that she must not run off from him. Once again, he embraced his child and allowed her to feel the safety of being in his arms. The child had been found by her abba.

We are all that little girl. Our sin and failures have left us crying in the street, lost, and searching for our loving father. We have all let go of his hand and run off on our own from time to time—which only ever leads us to fear. Yes, we need correction and to be rebuked from time to time, but that does not negate his love. In fact, it is out of his love that he does correct us. God is ready, waiting, and willing to throw his arms around you and tell you that you are loved. Nothing will stop him from reaching you if you just call out his name. "Abba! Abba!" You cannot be too far gone, have strayed too far away, or made too many mistakes for him to give up on you. You are his beloved child, the apple of his eye. He's got your picture in his wallet. He can't help but smile when he thinks about you, which is always. He will do anything to get to you. You mean that much to him. He wants to embrace you and allow you to feel the comfort and security of his endless love. He wants to look directly into your eyes and tell you that you are safe with him, and you always will be.

I will finish up this chapter with powerful words from Romans 8:31–39.

> What then shall we say to these things? If God is for us, who can be against us? He who did not spare his own Son but gave him up for us all, how will he not also with him graciously give us all things? Who shall bring any charge against God's elect? It is God who justifies. Who is to condemn? Christ Jesus is the one who died—more than that, who was raised—who is at the right hand of God, who indeed is interceding for us. Who shall separate us from the love of Christ? Shall tribulation, or distress, or persecution, or famine, or nakedness, or danger, or sword? As it is written, "For your sake we are being killed all the day long; we are regarded as sheep to be slaughtered." No, in all these things we are more than conquerors through him who loved us. For I am sure that neither death nor life, nor angels nor rulers, nor things present nor things to come, nor powers, nor height nor depth, nor anything

else in all creation, will be able to separate us from the
love of God in Christ Jesus our Lord.

There is nothing that will separate you from the love of God.
Let me establish a very important premise: it's not about you, but
it's about God's love for you and what Christ did for you on the
cross. You are loved. You have a heavenly father who cherishes you.
You have an Abba. All that is asked of you is that you believe it.

2

Mine

I AM DIVORCED. THAT is a sentence that I never thought I would ever have to write in my life. I have seen a lot of divorce in my life. Prior to my marriage, my parents, sister, aunts, uncles, cousins, and friends had all been divorced. I was determined that would never happen to me. Yet, here I am, divorced after a two-year marriage.

I can still remember the day that my now ex-wife told me that she no longer wanted to be married to me. I remember the day when the papers came in the mail when she filed to end what I thought would last our lifetimes. I will never forget the day that our divorce became final, our union was officially dissolved, and our connection forever broken. Please, do not read any of this as me placing the blame on her. There was fault on both sides. I say all of that because I want to talk about the emotion that comes with being rejected.

None of us do well with rejection. It is the exact opposite of the thing which we desire most in life, acceptance. From a young age, we begin to crave the acceptance of those around us. Once we start school, our desire is to be liked by our peers. That never goes away. Think about all the ways, while growing up, that you changed who you were to fit in with someone. My great love affair with coffee started this way.

I had joined the high school track team my junior year and began to befriend a classmate by the name of Alan. It just so happened that Alan and his family started coming to my church around the same time. Every Sunday, after service, Alan would grab a cup of joe at the coffee station (which have become as traditional to churches as steeples), and we would head off to Sunday school. I had never had any desire to drink that bitter brew prior to meeting him; however, I wanted to be liked by Alan. He was cool, funny, and popular. So, clearly, I needed to start drinking coffee like him. Because of my deep, unending desire to be accepted then, there isn't a day that goes by now that I don't consume at least one cup of the good stuff.

That is a very benign story of changing oneself to fit in. Many have ruined their lives doing it. There is something in the innermost part of ourselves that craves for those around us to say, "I like them!" This is why so many of us have become "yes" women and men. No matter what it is that someone asks of us, even if it greatly inconveniences us, we will unhesitantly say, "Yes." It doesn't matter how much we would much rather say, "No." This is the same reason why so many people, who want to be perceived as nice, get pushed around by others. This is also how so many charities guilt you into giving them your money. Don't get me wrong, these things can be good. It's all about the heart behind them. If your goal is to do good simply to do good, then have at it. If you want to do good so that others around you perceive you as "good," then you have a heart issue.

We all keep doing and doing and doing to try to gain acceptance and avoid rejection. Blaise Pascal, a seventeenth-century philosopher, wrote in his book *Pensées*:

> What else does this craving, and this helplessness, proclaim but that there was once in man a true happiness, of which all that now remains is the empty print and trace? This he tries in vain to fill with everything around him, seeking in things that are not there the help he cannot find in those that are, though none can help, since this

infinite abyss can be filled only with an infinite and im-
mutable object; in other words, by God himself.[1]

We keep searching for the approval and acceptance of people.
We keep looking to them for fulfillment and happiness. Some can
offer such things, but only temporarily. The ironic thing is that
what we are searching for is perpetually offered to us by our heavenly father. So, why are we not so apt to accept it? It goes back to
rejection.

We have all been rejected somewhere along the way, and it
probably happened pretty early on in our lives. I remember one
summer night when I was a kid, probably around the age of nine
or ten, and I was at a neighbor's house playing hide and seek. I had
found a perfect hiding place. As I would soon learn, I was hidden
a little too well. The group I was playing with was full of the "cool"
kids from my class. I had no reason to suspect that I didn't fit in
perfectly well with this group. I was lying underneath my neighbor's family's camper. I was being perfectly still because I could
hear the others coming near. At this point, I was doing all that I
could to control my breathing. I wanted to avoid being found at all
costs. They were closing in on me. In fact, I could even hear what
they were saying. That is precisely when I first found out the cruel
pain that comes with rejection. Their discussion was about why
I was there. They said that I didn't belong with them and wasn't
a cool kid, and they didn't even care if they found me. My heart
broke. I continued to lie there in a darkness that had nothing to do
with the night.

A little later on, when the game was over, I emerged with
tears streaming down my cheeks. They asked what was wrong, and
I told them that I had heard what they had said. Of course, they
began to cover their tracks. They claimed to know that I was under
there and were saying those things as a joke. I knew that this was a
lie, but I said that I believed them, dried my eyes, and went home.
I don't know that I have ever shared that story with anyone. For
those who were there, it is probably a distant memory that faded

---

1. Pascal, *Pensées*, 75.

from their minds a long time ago. For me, it set me off on a path of constantly feeling *less than*. I believe that it was in that moment that self-consciousness began to manifest itself in my life. A moment of rejection never lasts for only a moment.

Since that time, if you were to watch my life, you would never know the fractures in my self-image that were established that day. From the outside looking in, you would see a confident, outgoing person who has been successful in life. In high school, I went on to be an all-state football player, an award-winning playwright and actor, I did well in school, I had lots of friends, and I loved being the life of the party. After that, I went on to college and have given myself to youth ministry ever since. It is not uncommon for me to speak in front of large crowds and to come off as if I know what I am talking about. Even still, to this day, those feelings of being less than have yet to dissipate. Each and every rejection transports me back under that camper, being told that I am not good enough. My divorce brought all those emotions back to the surface in a much more powerful way.

I imagine that we all have had those moments. Those seminal memories of being rejected. We suppress them down as best that we can, but they are a beast that can only be caged for so long. Something will come along, such as: a lost friendship, being fired, being turned down from a job, a failed dream, a breakup or divorce, the failure of your child, etc., that will unlock that cage. Your mind will be flooded with the incessant requiem of, "Failure! Failure! Failure!" Your heart will ache, and your soul will cry out in anguish. Unfortunately, this is simply life. It could even be said that we move from rejection to rejection with intermittent moments of acceptance in between.

Subconsciously, we then start to apply this to our relationship with God. We allow the man or woman in the mirror, who tells us that we're not good enough, to become the voice of God. Because we often only see ourselves as our shortcomings, we imagine that is how God sees us as well. This simply is not true, at least if you choose to hold scripture as truth. In the Holman Christian Standard Bible, Romans 15:7 reads, "Therefore accept one another, just as the Messiah also accepted you, to the glory of God." Stop and think about the middle part of that verse, "Just as the Messiah accepted you . . . " You are accepted by Christ, every part of you. You may say, "But, I'm not good enough. I have made too many mistakes. I'm a failure. He would never want anything to do with someone like me." My friends, I hope that you do not get too offended at this next statement, but your opinion simply does not matter in this. Nobody is loved because they choose to be loved; they are loved because someone has chosen to love them. God has chosen to love and accept you, period. That's all that there is to it. "For the Lord is good; his steadfast love endures forever, and his faithfulness to all generations" (Psalm 100:5). The love that endures forever is the love that he has for you. You are not loved and accepted because you are perfect; no, you are loved and accepted because God loves you and accepts you, just as you are. The failures and rejections of your life have no say in any of this. I imagine that God was looking down on me, lying under that camper many years ago, as I was feeling the weight of inferiority for the first time and saying to me:

> Oh, my dear, beloved child, heed not their words. You are not what they say. I wonderfully and fearfully knit you together in your mother's womb. I have written your name in my book of life. I sent my son to die for you so that you may never taste true rejection. I accept you from now until forevermore. Do not listen to the names that they call you. Instead, listen to the name that I call you— *mine.*

Those are the words that God speaks over you every time that your heart breaks due to the agony of rejections. You are not what the world says you are. You are not your failures nor your sins. You are not inferior nor unlovable. You are his, you are loved, and his love endures forever.

A scene of worldly rejection plays out in the beginning of John 8. You probably know the story by the name of *The Woman Caught in Adultery.* If you don't, allow me to summarize. Jesus was teaching a crowd in the temple courts (the area surrounding the

Temple), as he often did. All of a sudden, he was interrupted by a group of Pharisees and teachers of the law who came storming in with an agenda. In this mob of pompous men, there was a lone, frightened woman. They forced her in front of the entire crowd, and all their eyes were fixed upon her. Then they turned to Jesus and said, "Teacher, this woman was caught in the act of adultery." I'm going to pause the story there and explain a couple things.

If you are unaware, adultery is the act of having sex where at least one of the participants is married to someone else. This crime was punishable by death in those times. Notice that they tell Jesus that she was "caught in the act," meaning that this was not some mere accusation, but she was, in fact, found while doing the deed. This leads to a few implications.

One, they probably did not allow this woman to get dressed before they brought her before Jesus. So, as she stands in front of that crowd, at best she has a blanket; at worst, she's completely na-ked, with nothing to cover her body or her shame. Two, in order to catch someone breaking the law, as adultery was, they must have at least two eyewitnesses as stated in Deuteronomy 19:15. I don't imagine that this horde of men was going from house to house, bedroom to bedroom and checking marriage licenses. They must have known that this was going to happen. They must have set her up to be used as collateral damage in their war with Jesus. That's the whole reason that this event came to pass. They wanted to trap Jesus, just as they trapped this woman. This is seen when one of the pious men poses this question, "In the law, Moses commanded us to stone such women. Now what do you say?" The religious lead-ers thought that they were clever because no matter what answer Jesus chose, he was going to be wrong. If he decided against the stoning, then Jesus would be against upholding the law and seen as a heretic. If he was in favor of letting the woman die, then he was not all-loving and compassionate. This would have been the end of Jesus' ministry, or so they thought.

Quick question, where was the man? It takes two to tango. Yet, it was only the woman who was brought forth for judgement. My thought on this is simple: the man was a co-conspirator with the "holy" men who had orchestrated this charade of upholding God's word. I am even willing to assume that he was a member of the group.

As the woman stood there, naked and afraid for her life, she was unaware of whom it was that was standing next to her. She knew that she was about to die. Her sin had led her to ultimate rejection by the people. Then, Jesus did something peculiar. He bent down and started writing in the sand. The men kept peppering him with questions about this woman's fate, but Jesus just kept writing in the sand. We have no earthly idea what he wrote. You will hear different theories espoused, but nothing can be for certain because scripture simply does not tell us. I don't think that it is all too important to know what he wrote. The importance lies in what happened as he wrote. The crowd's eyes would have begun to shift from the frightened woman to Jesus. Although it was for just a moment, she was freed from being the center of the unwanted attention. Next, Jesus stood up, and said these famous words, "Let him who is without sin among you be the first to throw a stone at her." Then, he bent back down and continued to write.

Slowly, one-by-one, each member of the crowd dropped his or her rock and walked away. Suddenly, there was no one around besides Jesus and the woman. A sinner with her savior. A creation with her creator. A daughter of God with the Son. Jesus finally stopped writing, lifted himself back up, and turned to the woman and asked, "Where are they? Has no one condemned you?" The woman looked around just to make sure that everyone had left. Seeing that all the crowd had departed, and the stones that were meant to kill her were lying on the ground, she responded, "No one, sir." Jesus said to her, "Neither do I condemn you; go, and from now on sin no more," freeing her from her guilt, shame, and rejection.

Yes, Jesus made a point to tell her to give up her life of sin. However, he did not cast the stone that he would have fully been justified in doing. It was the law, after all. Even by his own criteria, being without sin, he would have had the right to administer judgement. That is not who Jesus is, though. If you read the story carefully, you'll notice that he never even picked up a stone. Punishment never crossed his mind, only forgiveness.

When he stood next to this broken woman, he did not see what the world saw. The world saw her only for her shortcomings. It's fitting that she is not given a name in this story. I'm sure that she had to have had one. The Pharisees and the teachers of the law didn't care about her name, though. They saw her simply as a means to an end. "Who cares if she has to die in order for us to get what we want," must have been the thought running through their heads. She was meaningless to them.

I also find it appropriate that Jesus doesn't call her by name either. I am positive that he knew it, just as he knows each of ours. In the end, he gives her a new name— *mine*. Where the world and the religious leaders saw a sinner, Christ saw someone for whom he would go to the cross. By accepting the woman as his own, he freed her from the death that would have happened in only a moment if he had not stepped in for her. He freed her from the judgement of those who looked upon her and only saw moral failure. Ultimately, he freed her from the ramifications of rejection.

From the moment that she walked out of the temple courts and made her way back home, she was a new woman. Those who saw the ordeal play out and those who would later hear about it may have never let her forget her failures. It didn't matter because every time that she was reminded of her sin, she would always have the memory of standing next to Immanuel, God with us, and hearing him say, "Neither do I condemn you." She no longer had to fear rejection because, in that moment, she was accepted by Christ.

Her story is our story. We do not need to fear rejection when we have been accepted by our loving father through the work of the loving son. Worldly rejection is going to be commonplace in each of our lives. We will be told that we are not good enough far more times than we will want to hear it. Our past sins, mistakes, and failures will be thrown into our faces every day. Remember with whom it is that you are standing. Christ is by your side, always. He makes that promise to us in Matthew 28:20, "And behold, I am with you always, to the end of the age."

He is there in both our good and bad times. Whenever it is that you feel the walls closing in on you and you look out and all that you see is a crowd holding stones, know that Jesus is there, ready to bend down and begin writing. He will happily take all the attention of rejection and bear it on his broad shoulders. The world cannot convict what Christ has said he does not condemn. That is what is offered to us by our savior.

Rejection makes us feel just as vulnerable as the woman caught in adultery must have felt, standing there naked and guilty. Rejection breaks you and destroys your self-image. It makes you start to see yourself as *less than*. I felt every bit of that whenever my marriage disintegrated. We do such a great job of hiding it. We pretend that everything is ok. We say things like, "Time heals all wounds," "I need to pick myself back up and dust myself off," or "I just need to put on a brave face." These clichés are not helpful. In fact, they are harmful. They put the entire onus upon us to heal what we cannot. The hurt that you feel is real. Please, stop pretending otherwise. You may put on a smile each morning when you leave the house, just as you put on your shoes, but deep down, you know that it's all a lie.

The first step in overcoming the rejection in our lives is to go to the one who accepts us unconditionally. If that's not how you view God, then you need to adjust that image. We all need to stop seeing God as the one holding the stone and see him as the one who frees us from condemnation. You are not your sin, mistakes, shortcomings, or failures. You are not what the world says you are. You are God's child—loved and accepted, just as you are.

The founder of the United Methodist Church, John Wesley, penned what has come to be known as *A Covenant Prayer*. My favorite line in the prayer reads, in reference to the Father, Son, and Holy Spirit, "Thou art mine, and I am thine."[2] In modern English, it would go, "You are mine, and I am yours." That is the relationship with God that we have been offered, not one that is built upon completing a holy to-do list. If we want to escape the crippling anxiety that rejection creates in our lives, then we must accept that

2. Hamilton, *Revival*, 139.

we are God's, and he is ours. We need to move from seeing ourselves as condemned to seeing ourselves as free. Whenever you are told that you are a sum of your worst moments, remember these words spoken by Martin Luther:

> So, when the devil throws your sins in your face and declares that you deserve death and hell, tell him this: "I admit that I deserve death and hell, what of it? For I know one who suffered and made satisfaction on my behalf. His name is Jesus Christ, Son of God, and where he is there I shall be also."[3]

Jesus came, died, and suffered condemnation on your behalf. He endured ultimate rejection so that you would have eternal acceptance. Now he sits on his heavenly throne, saying the words, "Neither do I condemn you." There is no stone in his hand, only a hole.

3. Luther, *Luther: Letters of Spiritual Counsel*, 86–87.

3

Waiting and Watching

DURING THE FIRST FEW months of the COVID-19 pandemic, which we thought would only last a few weeks, the church staff where I work decided to livestream daily devotionals. The premise was simple, one of us would share something that we had read, and then we would all discuss it. This meant that we would all do a lot of talking over that time span. One of my issues is that I often speak before I think. Sometimes, I would say something and then have to decide if I agreed with it. That happened one particular morning when we were discussing the parable of the prodigal son. With little forethought, I uttered the declarative statement that, "We can learn all that there is to know about God by reading that parable." Then I began to wonder if what I said was philosophical or blasphemous, which do not reside far from each other. After thinking about it for a while, I decided that, for the most part, I agreed with myself. It's nice to have your own support.

The parable of the prodigal son is perhaps Jesus' most famous parable. To set the scene, Jesus was teaching a large crowd. It tells us at the beginning of Luke 15 that a crowd consisting of tax collectors, sinners, pharisees, teachers of the law, as well as his disciples had gathered around Jesus. He had with him what was considered the best of the best and the worst of the worst. He taught the crowd three parables that day. The first two were the parable of the lost sheep and the parable of the lost coin. Both of these use the example of someone going out and seeking something of great value which they have lost. These two parables illustrate that we are of great value to God, and that he seeks us out to bring us into relationship with him.

Then, Jesus began to teach about the prodigal son. This parable differs from the other two. Jesus used parables to teach something about God by using a real-life, human analogy. He explained this in Matthew 13, saying that he used parables because the people would not be able to understand the "heavenly" knowledge any other way. These teachings were always used to make a point about God. As I stated during that live-stream devotion, I believe that we can learn all that we need to know about God through the parable of the prodigal son.

This story began with a man and his two sons. The younger one came to his father and demanded that his father give him his inheritance, and, amazingly, the father gave it to him. This is a big deal. According to the inheritance law set in Deuteronomy 21:17, the younger son is entitled to one third of everything that the father owns. This included not only money, but cattle and other livestock, land, and possessions as well. Just like that, the father had given away a third of everything that he owned, and we learn from the story that this was a wealthy man. It is implied that the son went and sold everything that he had received so that he would just have the cash. The son no longer wanted anything to do with his father. He just wanted to set himself up nicely so he could go live life the way that he desired.

Imagine how the father had to have felt. His own son didn't care for him for more than what he could give him. He disowned and abandoned his own family because he wanted something more out of life. The father had to be angry, but more than that, he had to be heartbroken as he watched his son walk down the road for what he assumed would be the last time, never knowing if he would see him again.

The son then went off and lived the life that he coveted. He moved to a different country, spending his money wildly and living the high life. That is what the word "prodigal" actually means, to spend money recklessly. Life was good for the son. He had everything that he craved, lots of friends, and every desire of his heart. Unfortunately, his money ran out. When his money disappeared, so too did all of his friends. Suddenly, he found himself left with nothing. Then a famine hit the country in which he was living. The scripture says in verse 14 that, "He began to be in need." What that is really saying is that he was starving to death. He no longer had any means for food, and verse 16 says that, "No one gave him anything." He did what he had to do and took a job as a pig feeder.

I don't think that any of us would ever desire to have the job of a pig feeder. I'm sure that it was a dirty, gross job, but there is even more meaning behind this job for the son. Pigs were considered to be unclean, and according to Deuteronomy 14:8, Jews were forbidden from even touching them. This man was, not too long ago, a member of a prominent, wealthy, Jewish family. He had everything that he would ever need in life. He had plenty of food, a roof over his head, and a father who deeply loved him and took care of him. Now, he had nothing. He had given up everything about who he was and what he believed. He had gone down a path that he never imagined for himself. He just wanted to go and live life his way.

That is the first point of this parable. At the time that Jesus first told this parable, the prodigal son represented the tax collectors and sinners. Today, he represents us. He is actually one of two people in this story that represents us. We all fall into one of two camps in this parable, and sometimes, we fall into both. The first camp is that we have wandered down a path that we never intended. We have told our heavenly father that we don't need to live life the way that he desires for us, and we think we are better off figuring things out on our own and living it the way that we desire. That is what sin is, us saying to God that we know better than him and that our ways are better than his. That never ends up good for us.

Sin is coated in deception. There's a reason that we keep falling into sin even though we know better, and it's because it always looks good. The son had everything that he ever needed, but he was tempted by a life that promised to be better. Sin will never live up to its promise. We will all end up just like the son eventually. We will look around, feeling broken, hurt, and lonely, and wonder how we got to that point. How did what once looked so enticing turn out to be so deceptive? Then we will begin scrambling to try to put the pieces back together on our own, much like the son did when he hired himself out to feed the pigs. We will continue to compromise who we are to try to fix our lives, only to continue further down that path on which we don't want to be. We will be afraid to go back to our father because we are ashamed of what we have done. Are you currently on that path in your life? I urge you to search your heart and examine your life. Are there parts that you are trying to hide from others and from God? Are there parts that you keep secret because you know that they're not the way that God desires for you to live? Don't keep going down that path. Don't keep hiding from God. Instead, make the same choice the prodigal son is about to make in the parable.

After working with the pigs for a while, the son realized that things were not getting better. He was still starving. It says that he desired to eat what the pigs were eating. He finally came to his senses and realized that this is not the way that life should be. He decided to go back to the place where he was safe, taken care of, and loved. He decided to return to his father.

However, he was embarrassed and ashamed because of what he had done. He didn't believe that he could go back to his father as a son. Instead, he was going to plead with his father to hire him as a worker. Although he didn't believe that he could go back to the same relationship that he had once had, he could at least be a servant and be fed. So that's what he did. He even prepared a speech to say when he would meet his father again. Now, this is something that I am sure many of us can relate to in our pasts. I can think of plenty of times growing up when I knew that I was in trouble, so I had my speech prepared. I would typically go one of two ways with it: either I was prepared to explain how it was definitely not my fault, or I was going to be so contrite that whomever I was confessing to would have pity on me. Either way, the goal was to get myself out of the punishment for what I had done. The younger son prepared to go the route of contrition with his speech. He knew that he was guilty, and he was just hoping for the best.

As he walked down the road to go back to his father's house, his dad saw him while he was still a "long way off" (Luke 15:20). This part of the story always brings me to tears. Do you know why his dad saw him while he was a long way off? It's because he had been looking for him and waiting for him to return home from the moment that he left. The father loved his son. He would sit on his porch for day after day and hour after hour, hoping and waiting to see his son come back to him. When the father finally did see his son, he didn't wait for him to reach the house. Verse 20 says, "he felt compassion and ran," to his son. What you may not know is that it was considered highly undignified for an older man, especially a wealthy landowner, to run. *He didn't care.* There was only one thing that he cared about in that moment, and that was to get to his son as fast as he could and throw his arms around him and welcome him home. That's exactly what he did. As his father approached him, the son began to go into his speech, telling his father that he didn't deserve to be called his son anymore. The father wasn't having any of it, cut his speech off, and called for the servants to bring the finest clothes to dress the son and prepare for a feast to celebrate. One of the articles of clothing that the father called for was a ring to put on the son's hand. This ring would have had the family seal on it, and by placing it on the son's hand, it showed that he was a member of the family again.

To me, this is the most powerful image in all of scripture. The son had come back home a broken man. He was guilty, and the father had every right to not want anything to do with him. But that's not who the father was because that's not who God is. First John 4:10 reads, "In this is love, not that we have loved God but that he loved us and sent his Son to be the propitiation for our sins." That is the love demonstrated here. The son had not loved his father well, but his father still deeply loved him. Most of us do not love God well, but he still deeply loves us— so much so that he sent his son to die for us. There is nothing, I repeat nothing, that you can do that will make God stop loving you. You cannot out sin God's love. You cannot outrun it. You cannot hide from it. You cannot escape how much the father loves you, no matter what. Christ paid the ultimate price so that we can experience God's love forevermore. Towards the end of his life, John Newton, the writer of *Amazing Grace*, said, "Although my memory's fading, I remember two things clearly: I am a great sinner and Christ is a great savior."[1] That's it, folks. There is no truer statement that will ever be said than that. God's love will always outweigh our sin.

Look at how the father treated his son when he came back home. God is going to treat us the exact same way. He's going to run to us, throw his arms around us, and tell us that we are so deeply loved that it doesn't matter where we've been or what we've done; the only thing that matters is that we are back home with him. We have no need to run from him. The only thing that we need to do is run to him. He wants to throw that celebration because his child has come back to him. He's not going to chastise or disown you; he is going to love you.

I shared a personal story during that same devotion that I will share here as well. When I was a teenage boy, my chief concern in life was to impress girls. Admittedly, I was not very successful. One day, I was in a local store with my group of friends, which just so happened to have a girl in it with whom I was infatuated. I decided that I was going to shoplift a ring for her, so I slipped the ring into my pocket. Unfortunately for middle school Kyle, the shop owner was suspicious of us and was keeping an eye on what we were doing. He instantly noticed that the ring was taken but didn't know who took it. He confronted us. I was able to get the ring out of my pocket and drop it under the table behind me without him seeing me. Of course, once that happened, I told the owner that he could search my pockets and he would see that I didn't take the ring. He kicked us all out and banned us from ever coming back. I headed

1. Pollock, *Amazing grace: John Newton's story*, 182.

out of the store feeling good because I had dodged that bullet. It was smooth sailing from there . . . until the next day or two.

My dad has worked for the city that I grew up in since he was a teenager. He began washing police cars when he was in high school, then was a police dispatcher for years, and has worked for the city water and sewer department for about twenty years. He has also been a member of the volunteer fire department since he was a teenager, including a long stint as Deputy Fire Chief. Now, he is on city council. I tell you all of that to say that he was and is very well-connected in that town. My sister, brother, and I couldn't get away with anything because he would always find out about it. Most of the time, he would know about it before we ever got home.

I went to my dad's house, and he called me down to the base-ment and asked me if I had tried to shoplift the ring. I don't know who his informant was, but I had been turned in. Immediately, I broke down and began to cry and admitted my crime. I was prepared for the worst. My dad told me that he was disappointed in my decision and that I should have known better than that. Then he hugged me and told me that he loved me and to never do something like that again. My dad had no idea that, on that day, he would forever sear into my mind the image that I have of God whenever I have been caught up in my sin and mistakes. Whenever I am confessing and asking for forgiveness, I am always transported back into that basement. Except now, I am with my heavenly father, but the scene always plays out the same way.

That is why we don't need to run from God. He is not against us; He is for us. He may be disappointed in our choices, but he is always going to embrace us, forgive us, and tell us that he loves us. Why do we run? Brennan Manning wrote in his book *Abba's Child*, "Define yourself radically as one beloved by God. This is the true self. Every other identity is an illusion."[2] You are God's child. You are loved. And nothing will ever separate you from that love, period. That is who you are. Do not listen to sin's lie that you are less than that. If you feel that God does not love you, then I chal-lenge you to go to him and feel his embrace. If we ever feel that we

2. Manning, *Abba's Child*, 60.

are separated from God, it is not our father who has run away from us. It is us who have run away from him. He is there watching and waiting for you to come home.

This parable ends with a conversation between the older son and the father. The older son was upset that the father was making such a big deal about the younger son returning. He told his father that he had always done what was right and had stuck with his father his whole life. If anyone deserved to have the fattened calf killed and a celebration thrown in his honor, it was him. The older son was suffering from self-righteousness. When Jesus told this parable, the older son represented the Pharisees and the teachers of the law. Once again, this is now representing us. This is the other camp I alluded to earlier into which we sometimes fall. We have been doing our best to live life the way that God desires for us, yet we become jealous of how God is blessing other people. We feel we deserve more in life than what God has given us.

The father didn't rebuke or get mad at the older brother; instead, he responded with love. He told him, "all that is mine is yours" (Luke 15:31). The older brother would still receive his reward. In those times when jealousy has crept into our lives and turned us self-righteous, we need to be reminded that everything that God has promised us is still ours. We will receive our reward and crowns in heaven. Sometimes, we have to lay our ego aside and rejoice in the work that God is doing in others' lives as well. There is room enough in the father's house for those who were lost but have been found and those who have strived to walk with God all of their days. It's not about us. It's about God and the wonderful redemptive work that he is doing in the lives of all of his children.

As I stated earlier, this parable is all that you need to know about God. Admittedly, that was a bit facetious. God is so complex that I could spend the rest of eternity trying to explain him and still not have enough time. I will tell you this, though: if all you knew about God came from this parable, then you would have a great understanding of who he is, and it is that, as 1 John 4:8 tells us, "God is love." God is love, and God loves you— no matter what. You are his beloved child. You cannot escape his love. All we ever need to do is go to him, and he will come running to us. It's not because of who we are but because of whose we are, and we are his! He loves us because we are his children.

Is your heart hurting or broken? Is it tired or weary? Is it heavy from the weight that you've been carrying around for far too long? If so, then I implore you to go to your heavenly father. Let him speak lovingly to you. Let him speak directly to your heart. He wants to tell you how much you are adored and cherished. He wants to tell you that he has not turned his back on you. He wants to invite you to lay down all of your guilt and shame, never to be picked back up again. If this sounds like what you need, then go to one who loves beyond comprehension. He is there— watching and waiting for you to come home— so that he can throw his arms around his beloved child.

4

Hide and Seek

As I HAVE STATED previously, I am divorced. This came as a shock to me, and I knew that it would be shocking to everyone else as well. As far as anyone could tell, from the outside looking in, we had the perfect life together. We seemed to be happy and deeply in love. No one could see the cracks that were slowly forming that led to the demise of the marriage. This was mostly due to the fact that I only let people see what I wanted them to see when it came to my personal life. It didn't matter what was going on; I was always going to tell everyone that everything was great. You see, I suffer greatly from the delusion that I need to be perfect. I have always covered up and masked any issues in my life because it would be crazy to allow people to see the chinks in my armor. My divorce was no different.

It was not until almost two months after my ex-wife asked for a divorce that I even told my parents. The only motivation for me telling them was because she had moved out and started to rent her own place. I figured that might be a little suspicious to them if they found out about it. The main reason that I hesitated so long was because I like to think of myself as the perfect son. I rarely got into trouble growing up and received plenty of accolades along the way. I took a lot of pride in the moments when my parents would say that they ran into someone and that person had talked about how good of a kid I was. I believed that I had an image I constantly needed to uphold. My marriage was the first major failure of my life. I was mostly worried that my perceived pristine image would forever be altered.

I told my mom first. I was fairly certain how she would react. She has always been my biggest fan and supported me, no matter what. I knew that she would immediately be on my side. She would defend me to the death, as any good mom would. I was totally correct in my assumption. She was shocked, but she firmly planted her flag in my camp. Then, it was time to tell my dad.

I was twenty-nine years old when I had to break the unfortunate news to him. I still remember making that phone call with trembling hands and a shaky voice. It took every bit of my strength to force the words to come out of my mouth that my wife had left me. Then, there was only a second or two before he responded, but it felt like an eternity. His response, at first, was one of total disbelief. After he processed the news, he did what any loving father would do— he had sympathy for his son. He alleviated all my fears with his compassion. He knew that his son was hurting and broken, and all he wanted to do was make me feel better. Why I was so scared, I will never know. My dad has always been there for me and has never given me a reason to doubt his love. Even as an adult, there's just something about a son not wanting to disappoint his father.

This beautiful scene in an ugly situation is one that has played out since the beginning of time, literally. Do you remember the story of Adam and Eve? If you don't, please allow me to summarize it. These were the first two people that God created. They lived a life of joy, splendor, and plenty in the Garden of Eden. It was just the two of them and God, in a perfect existence. They had everything they could ever need, and they only had to follow one rule, "But of the tree of the knowledge of good and evil you shall not eat, for in the day that you eat of it you shall surely die" (Genesis 2:17). Seems pretty simple. They had a wonderful life in the garden, until a pesky serpent showed up.

The serpent, who was Satan in disguise, came to Eve and asked her, "Did God actually say, 'You shall not eat of any tree in the garden'?" (Genesis 3:1). Eve responded by explaining to her new acquaintance that God told them that they could eat from any tree they wanted, just not the one in the middle or they would die. The clever serpent told her that she wouldn't die, and that God actually wanted them to eat from the tree. This was the first temptation in the history of the world. Eve fell prey to Satan's plan, and people haven't stopped giving into temptation since. After she ate the forbidden fruit, she took some to offer to Adam. Of course, as most men know, if a pretty girl asks you to do anything, you're going to say yes. Immediately, they both came to the realization that they were naked and were filled with guilt and shame. With one single act, both Adam and Eve went against what God had asked of them and brought forth the downfall of all mankind.

A little later on, God came to the garden for his evening stroll. This must have been something that he did regularly because the newly fallen creations recognized the sound of his walking. What had normally been a time of joyous communion with their creator had now become their greatest moment of fear. Genesis 3:8 tells us that Adam and Eve "hid" from God when they heard him draw near. Imagine that: they were now hiding from the one that had given them everything they had ever desired. God, excited to see his favorite handiwork, called out to them. Adam, seemingly still hiding behind some bush or tree, cried out, "I heard the sound of you in the garden, and I was afraid, because I was naked, and I hid myself." God replied, "Who told you that you were naked? Have you eaten of the tree of which I commanded you not to eat?" (Genesis 3:10–11). Adam and Eve then explained what had happened and confessed their sin. God gave them some consequences for their actions because sin will always have earthly consequences, but what happened next is astounding. God, knowing that Adam and Eve were feeling guilt and shame from being naked, made them clothing. This was the first act of grace (God's undeserved favor) that anyone had ever received. They deserved death— that was the stated repercussion for eating from the tree. Instead, God still loved them and provided them with what they needed.

How many times has this back and forth played out in your life? Maybe you haven't thought of it this way before, but this is the exact situation that we find ourselves living day-in and day-out. We often make fun of Adam and Eve for not following the one rule that God set for them. We say things like, "How could they eat from the tree when they knew that they weren't allowed? Idiots!" My friends, I cannot think of very many of God's rules that we don't break daily. Jesus even offers us a simplified list of commandments that is only to love God and love others. Even still, we fail far more often than we succeed. I can promise you that each of us would have eaten from that tree. If you think otherwise, then you have too lofty of a view of yourself.

We all fall prey to sin and Satan's craftiness every day. I doubt that I have to spend too much time convincing you that you are a sinner. Paul put it this way in Romans 3:23, "For all have sinned and fall short of the glory of God." He then informs us in Romans 6:23 that the consequence of sin has not changed since God first created the rule about the tree of knowledge of good and evil, "For the wages of sin is death." We know the cost of sin, but yet we still fall victim to it every day. The worst part is what happens after we have gone against what God desires for us— we hide.

We become just like Adam and Eve in the garden. We don't want anything to do with God. We think that if we just avoid him, everything will be ok. That is pure lunacy. To think that we can hide from God is a fallacy. David addressed this idea in Psalm 139. In verse 7, he asked the questions, "Where shall I go from your Spirit? Or where shall I flee from your presence?" He goes on to explain that there is nowhere for him to go that escapes the presence of God. Our hiding is futile, and it only hurts us. As we try to hide from God, we separate ourselves from our sustainer. We build a chasm between us and our creator. God has only ever been good to us, yet we think that we are better off running from him than going to him. Why do we do this?

It's because, just like the two people in the garden, we are afraid. God had never given Adam and Eve any reason to be afraid of him. He had only showered them with love up until the point of their giving into temptation. This is what sin does in our lives. It makes us afraid to show God our true, naked selves. We are afraid to be vulnerable with God. We think that he won't love us the same way if he were to see all of our baggage. We all have the same syndrome that I struggle with, seeing ourselves as the perfect child. We think that if we continue to put on airs and only let God in on the good stuff, he will never know of all the things with which we are struggling. He won't know about those lustful, prideful, or hateful thoughts. He will never be aware of how we gossiped about family or coworkers. Besides, can God even read text messages? It's best if we never explain to him that we had a chance to do something good for someone else, but we chose ourselves over that person. We like the idea that God should operate on a need-to-know basis, and all that we will ever reveal to him is the good side of us with a quick "forgive me of my sins" tacked on the end. Our naivety should be most pitied. David addressed this as well in Psalm 139: 1–4:

> O Lord, you have searched me and known me! You know when I sit down and when I rise up; you discern my thoughts from afar. You search out my path and my lying down and are acquainted with all my ways. Even before a word is on my tongue, behold, O Lord, you know it altogether.

God knows every single one of our failings and faults. We need to stop thinking we can hide from him.

One of the coolest parts of the Genesis 3 story is when God entered into the garden. He was expecting to see the first of his children, but they were nowhere to be found. God didn't just go about his business or leave a note; instead, he called out to them. That was the first game of hide and seek that was ever played. God still searched for them. He knew what they had done because he is and has always been all-knowing. He knew that they had defied him and had eaten from the tree. They broke his trust and turned their backs on him. He didn't care. He knew exactly what they were feeling and experiencing. For the first time in their lives, they felt the pain of failure. Before they ever had any clothing, they had dirty laundry. This did not disqualify them from being sought after by God. He still desperately wanted to be with them. It was not God who was distant from them. This is the same for us today. God seeks you out. He knows exactly what you have done. He knows every mistake and sinful thought. He knows which forbidden fruits you have eaten. He still seeks you out anyways. He is not a fickle god. He is a God who is incomprehensibly faithful to his people. He is the Father who stands by his child's side— regardless of the situation.

Every time that you try to hide behind a bush or a tree because you are afraid that God may see you in your nakedness, he is still going to draw near to you. He's going to call out to you, "Where are you my beloved child? I have come to be with you." We must get rid of this false narrative that states that God only wants to be with perfect people. None of us would have a shot if that was the truth. Adam and Eve were in the throes of their sinfulness, and he sought them out. Their failures did not disqualify them from being in the presence of their loving father, and neither do yours.

Whenever we feel far away from God, it is often because we are holding something back from him. There is something that we have decided is too big for him to handle, or maybe we think that it is too much for him. We can easily develop a warped mindset that creates a god who only wants our good deeds. That is not who God is, nor is it who he will ever be. God asks for one thing and one thing only—you. All of you. God didn't see Adam and Eve's nakedness and turn away. He didn't say, "Look at you! Look at how your blunder has ruined your life. You're standing there, naked and afraid. I do not want anything to do with you." He instead offered them love and grace.

Before that happened, God did give them consequences for their actions. Sin will always have earthly consequences. You cannot live your life in a way which goes against what God has desired for you and expect it to be all rainbows and cupcakes. As it was stated in the first half of Romans 6:23, "For the wages of sin is death . . . " That does not only mean an ultimate, physical death. It also means that there will be some sort of other death along the way. Maybe the death ends up being the death of your peace or happiness, maybe it's the death of a friendship or marriage, maybe it's the death of your financial stability or job security. There are a lot of ways in which our sin creates deaths in our lives along the way. We have all felt it and dealt with it. I can promise you this: the consequence will never be the death of the Father's love for you.

The second half of Romans 6:23 is, " . . . But the free gift of God is eternal life in Christ Jesus our Lord." Because of what Christ did for each of us on the cross, we have been saved from the everlasting death, which is an eternity separated from God. Earthly consequences are necessary for us to learn our lesson. Every parent knows that their children need to be disciplined in order to grow up as well-adjusted adults. In fact, some of the most maladjusted people in this world became that way because they grew up without consequences for their actions. Good and proper discipline is administered out of love, not the lack of it. So, when facing the ramifications of your sins, know that it is not an indication that you have been disqualified from God's love. We see that play out in the lives of the original sinners.

After God decreed what would happen as a result of their malfeasance, he did something that they could not have expected. They had to be feeling as down as they possibly could. Prior to eating the fruit, guilt and sadness had yet to be experienced. Now, they were filled with both. On top of that, they had just found out that their lives were going to get significantly more difficult as a result of their sin. For Eve, childbirth was going to be much more painful. Adam was informed that he was going to have to work significantly harder to grow and harvest food. As a final stipulation, they got kicked out of Eden. This was undoubtedly the lowest moment of their lives. Genesis 3:21 reads, "And the Lord God made for Adam and his wife garments of skins and clothed them." They were feeling every bit of their shame as they stood there naked. God did not leave them in that state. Not only did he make them clothing, but he also put the clothing on them. He saw the effect that sin had had on them. He saw the brokenness and hurt in their eyes. He knew that they were crushed in spirit. So, he did something about it.

God will never leave us in our brokenness. He cares for us way too much for that. He's going to look down upon you and see you when you are at your lowest and provide you with whatever it is that you need. Your sin will never strip you of the love with which God has clothed you. The vulnerability that the nakedness of guilt and shame brings upon us has forever been covered by the blood of the lamb.

The account of Adam and Eve's lives does not end there. They go on to have children (there's a whole to-do with their first two sons) and become the parents of all mankind. What is most amazing about their story is that they lived out the rest of their days in relationship with God. They really messed up everything; however, God never stopped loving them. You think your sin is bad? Compare it to bringing about the fall of all of creation. If that is not enough to make God stop loving you, then I don't know what is.

We are so afraid of disappointing God that we try to hide our true and authentic selves from him. We're afraid to let him in on who we really are. The crazy thing is that he knows every detail about each and every one of us and still loves us. There is no reason to be afraid. We may have to suffer consequences for our sins, but they never separate us from the one who is always drawing near to us. There is no need to play hide and seek because you will never win. Besides, all that it does is bring more pain and hurt. He will handle us just as he handled Adam and Eve. He will love us, take care of us, cover our guilt and shame, provide us with what we need, and invite us to live out the rest of our days in relationship with him. He comes into our lives every day because he is excited to be with his beloved children. We need not hide, nor be afraid. We need to say, "Here I am, dad. I have something to tell you. I made a mistake today." Then, we get to experience his forgiveness and love.

I was so afraid to tell my dad about my divorce. It was silly of me. I thought that he may look at me differently. That did not cross his mind, not even for a second. All he saw was his son. That's exactly what God sees when we are at our lowest, his daughters and sons. He probably is not even very concerned with the details. His concern is that his children receive the compassion and love that they need. You can be vulnerable with him. Those worst parts of you are still parts that he loves. He loves you, *all of you*, just as you are. There's no need to run and hide from our heavenly father because he will seek you until he finds you, and when he does, he is going to pour his grace and love out upon you. All of who he is loves all of who you are.

Adam and Eve never spent a moment of their lives outside of God's love. From the instant that God formed Adam out of the dust and crafted Eve from a rib, they only knew of the affection of their creator. Even when Eve took that first bite and Adam followed suit, they were not disowned by the Divine. As they hid themselves amongst the bushes or behind a tree, the Lord came looking for them. I'm sure that they must have doubted God's steadfastness after they bought Satan's lie. That is where all of his lies will lead us— into doubt. Even though they must have questioned how their father felt about them, God never wavered, even for a second, in his love for them. We can know that by how he treated them so gracefully. I am confident of one thing: Adam and Eve never again doubted God's love for them. Why? Because they were forgiven people. Each day, as they put on their clothes, it would serve as a reminder of that first time God clothed them. As they looked back on their memories of being in the garden, even in the pain of losing paradise, they would recall how God dealt kindly with them. We must do the same thing.

As I think about my divorce, I am confident that God never desired for it to happen. I am a firm believer that each marriage is meant to stand the test of time, but mine failed. As tragic and painful as it was, I have never felt God so near to me. He came into my garden one day, where I was hidden and ashamed, and called out, "Kyle, where are you?" I replied, "I heard you come near, Lord, and

I was afraid because I failed you." This is where the story changes for you and me. He does not reply with words of condemnation because we live in the age of grace which was ushered in with Jesus' death and resurrection. Instead, he says to us:

> My sweet, hurting child. Do not be afraid, for I am with you always. Do you not know that I love you? I sent my son to die for you, yes you, so that you would never have to doubt that. Come out from hiding, you have no reason to be scared. Come, let me hug you. I love you. I don't like that things did not go the way that I desired, but that's ok. Christ carried all your mistakes and failures with him to the cross. I see your heart, and I can see that it is broken. Come to me and let me heal it. You are my beloved creation in whom I am well pleased. You do not need to feel guilt and shame. There is no room for them while you are in your father's arms. Stay here as long as you need. Things will get better, I promise. Until then, let me love you just as you are. I am all that you need.

Those are the words that he speaks to each of us whenever life has fallen apart around us. It doesn't matter if it was your fault or not. God is not in the blame business. He is our loving father, and he wants to wipe away all of our tears. Just like when I was afraid to tell my dad about my divorce, the only thing I was delaying was feeling his love and compassion. God is for you, and he loves you. There is no need to run or hide. There is only more pain when you do. Instead, draw near to God as he draws near to you. Let him wrap his arms around you and comfort you. Do not be afraid. Run to him and allow yourself to be loved by your father. He is all that you need.

5

Enter the Throne Room

IN ISAIAH 6, AN interesting scene unfolds. The prophet was having a vision, and he was transported into the heavenly realm. It was truly a spectacular site. There were angels flying around and chanting. The whole house was filled with smoke. The floor shook in verse 3 whenever an angel called out, "Holy, holy, holy is the Lord of hosts; the whole earth is full of his glory!" Most importantly, the Lord was there, sitting on his throne. Isaiah had entered into the throne room of God. A place where no mortal man would ever dare tread. In fact, Isaiah was so blown away by what he saw, he began to shout about his unworthiness of being there. This was literally an other-worldly scene. Take a moment and picture what this must have looked like, and imagine that it was you standing there instead of Isaiah. I feel as though we would all be quick to mention how we do not belong there. Here's the thing: each of us is invited into that very same throne room whenever we would like. That is what happens when we start to pray. When we enter into the posture of prayer, we are spiritually transported from wherever we are in that moment to the presence of our father.

Prayer is a peculiar thing. Have you ever stopped and really thought about it? There you are at home, in your car, at church, at work, or wherever you may be, and you just start talking to God.

You don't even need to do it audibly. The craziest part is that he hears you! If someone had no concept of prayer, you would look like an insane person to them. God tells us in Jeremiah 29:12, "Then you will call upon me and come and pray to me, and I will hear you." God is always there to listen to us whenever we decide to go to him. In fact, he is always eagerly awaiting the next time that he gets to have a chat with you. We must never lose sight of God as our father. Like any good dad, he will always make time to talk with his children. He has not made the throne room unapproachable; instead, there is a sign that reads, "Come on in!" It is up to us to choose how often that we enter into his holy presence.

Throughout my years in ministry, when I have asked people where they most lack in their spiritual life, they almost always have said their prayer life. I think there are a couple reasons for this. First, we have made prayer out to be much more formal than it was ever meant to be. We hear those whom we deem as *good* at praying. You know the ones that I am talking about. They often find their way to a microphone or in front of a large crowd, and then they proceed to say a lengthy prayer where they quote a solid portion of the Bible and throw around words like "intercession" and "propitiation." The common person is no longer focused on being in a moment of prayer, but they are now questioning if they will ever be worthy of talking to God so beautifully. I don't mean to diminish those who can unfurl a magnificent prayer without any forethought. It is actually a wonderful thing. However, prayers are not judged by their eloquence but by their willingness. The only poorly said prayer is the one that is not said at all.

Whenever you are spending time with your earthly dad or talking with him on the phone, are you trying to impress him with your word choice? Is he more satisfied with you if you start speaking in Greek or Hebrew? When you finish does he say, "It was great talking to you, but you did not use enough four syllable words"? Of course not! His satisfaction is not in what you say or how you say it, but it is simply in spending time with you. That is exactly what prayer is, alone time with daddy. Shouldn't we all want that? I hear all the time from people who have lost their earthly fathers that they would give anything to just have one more conversation with them. How much more so should we desire to converse with our heavenly father? We need to move ourselves into the position of always desiring to be with him, not one of trying to impress him.

The second reason can be best explained by a story from my childhood. I was five years old when my parents got divorced. I don't remember it being a tragic time in my life. I honestly don't know if I fully comprehended what was going on at the time. I have very few memories as a kid of my family being all together. After their divorce, my father moved about a couple of miles away to live with his brother, and he remained a part of my daily life. My sister, brother, and I lived with my mom, but we would go over to my dad's place about every other day. At least that is how I remember it. Somewhere along the way, my dad had the idea that he would spend an entire day with each of us individually. I remember only a single, certain aspect of when it was my turn. It was not anything to do with what we did. I think that we probably went out to eat or something; I'm not sure. What I vividly remember was when it was time to go back home, and our day together had come to a close. I wept. I didn't want the day to end. I had had such a good time being with him. What we did on that day was not what mattered. What affected me was simply getting to spend a day alone with my dad. What a wonderful and heartwarming scene that must have been for him to see his son totally heartbroken at the mere thought that our day together had come to a close. That is the heart that we should have when it comes to spending time with our heavenly father. It should break our heart whenever we have to say amen and move on to the next thing.

We are so worried about checking the prayer box for the day that we just mutter something heartless and consider it completed. Imagine trying to maintain a relationship with somebody that you love by saying the same mundane thirty second speech to them every day. There would be no depth. This is why I think many of us struggle with our prayer lives; we simply do not place much importance upon it. There should be nothing that takes priority over our time spent alone with God. I'm not suggesting that we all spend eight hours a day in prayer, although that is not a bad idea either. There is nothing wrong with a short prayer on your commute to work, but I hope that isn't the only prayer that you say all day.

Checking in with God throughout the day is a great way to build up your prayer life. Yes, he knows everything that you're going through and thinking, but he still wants to hear about it anyways. First Thessalonians 5:17 tells us to, "Pray without ceasing." That is done by little prayers throughout the day. When you start feeling anxious, ask him to help you. When you've received some sort of blessing, thank him for it. When you see someone struggling, pray for them. When you are moved by how beautiful the sunset is, praise him for his work. It doesn't always need to be long, drawn-out prayers. Short, constant contact with the Father will often be a better way to stay connected to him throughout the day.

Prayer also needs to be honest. God doesn't need your clichés and platitudes. He doesn't need you to say things that you really don't believe. If you are deeply hurting inside, a prayer that tells him how thankful you are for everything going on in your life is not as useful as spilling your guts to him. Don't pray as you think you should; pray as you truly feel. David made a habit of this in the Psalms. Here's what he wrote is Psalm 10:1, "Why, O Lord, do you stand far away? Why do you hide yourself in times of trouble?" Does that sound much like David telling God that everything is ok? No, he was questioning why God had left him out to dry when he needed him. I do not speak for God, but I imagine that meant more to him than David writing, "Thanks God, everything is great." God wants your true, authentic self. Yet, we often try to hide what is on our heart from the one that knit it together.

There is one prayer in particular that I consider to be the most honest prayer that I have ever said. I was twenty-four at the time and working for a parachurch youth ministry called Young Life. I had been hired to move into a small, backwoods town in West Virginia and begin the ministry there. It had its ups and down, but I had hit a rut. Things were not going the way that I felt that they should be. I had in my mind how it needed to go and was nowhere near my goal. I thought that I was doing everything right and couldn't understand why the results weren't there. One evening, I had had it. I was so mad at everyone and everything for not falling into the image of success that I had created. I remember pulling into the parking lot of my apartment after what I had considered a failure of an event. I sat out in my vehicle with a stream of tears flowing down my cheeks. I decided that it was time that I had some words with God about the situation. I took a harsh and authoritative tone with him and said, "Why did you bring me here? Why on earth did you call me to this place? I'm doing everything that I possibly can, and it's not working! I'm so frustrated. Do you have any idea what you are doing?" I don't know exactly how God took my words. I like to think that he had a chuckle listening to them, but also felt compassion for his hurting child. I bore my heart to God in a way that I don't know that I had before then. He got all of me and all that I was feeling. He wasn't offended. God has big shoulders; he can handle whatever it is that we dish out. He's not going to stop loving you for telling him what you truly think. That's because that's how a real relationship works. There is freedom to express who you really are, and God loves who you really are. He has given each of us carte blanche to communicate that with him. Prayer needs to be genuine, intentional, and truthful. That is what God asks from you.

We should be greatly impacted by having been with our father through prayer. One would have to imagine that Isaiah was deeply affected by his vision of the throne room. I can relate to Isaiah and his vision. In 2020, I was at a youth conference called Resurrection in Pigeon Forge, Tennessee. On the final evening, everyone participated in a communion ceremony. Because of where my group was sitting, we were instructed to walk up in front of the stage to receive the bread and the grape juice. As I stood in line waiting for my turn, something spectacular happened. The smoke from the stage was pouring over to where I was standing. The beat of the kick drum reverberated in my chest with every strike. The band was loudly singing praises to God. All of a sudden, I was no longer standing in the conference center; I had been transported into the throne room. My mind envisioned everything that Isaiah had seen. I took communion and returned to my seat. I was shaken. I couldn't believe what I had felt and experienced in that moment. I have an immense appreciation for communion, but that one was different. I felt as though I was different afterwards. That is what is offered to us freely. The only thing that holds us back from entering the throne room is ourselves.

I think that many of us underestimate the power that is in prayer. We often hear the phrase, "The least that I can do is pray." We tend to treat prayer as a last resort, when in reality, it is our deadliest weapon. We have, at our disposal, the ability to call upon God to step in on our behalf. The supreme being, who created everything in the universe just by speaking, is willing to step into our lives and deal with our stuff. Jesus speaks to this in Mark 11:24, "Therefore I tell you, whatever you ask in prayer, believe that you have received it, and it will be yours." His brother reiterates this in James 4:2, "You do not have, because you do not ask." All that we have to do is ask for it, believe we will receive it, and it is ours. Those are the words in the Bible, some of which are red. How sad is it that we all miss out on blessings in life simply because we don't ask our father for them? When we don't call upon God in prayer for help, we are making ourselves Samson after his haircut.

Do you remember the story of Samson? His life is chronicled in Judges 13–16. Allow me to sum up a long, complex story. Samson was a judge of Israel, which was the country's ruling human authority at the time. Prior to his birth, God informed Samson's mom that he was to abstain from forbidden food and alcohol and to never cut his hair. In return, God blessed him with abnormal strength. Rumor has it that he was the strongest man to ever live. Things went well for the most part for Samson, even though he wasn't the most faithful Jew to ever live. Eventually, he fell in love with a woman from Philistine, which was a neighboring country that did not get along with Israel and worshipped a false god. Now, all throughout the Old Testament, God told the Jews not to marry foreign people who worshiped foreign gods. Also, all throughout the Old Testament are stories of Jews marrying foreign people who worshipped foreign gods. It typically didn't end well.

Samson and Delilah ended up getting hitched, despite the decree from God. The Philistinian leaders thought that maybe they could use her to trap Samson, since they couldn't defeat him in battle. They offered her a solid chunk of money, and she agreed. After a little playful back and forth between the two lovebirds, one of which was trying to sell her husband out to his enemies, Samson informed Delilah that his strength came from never having cut his hair. When Samson fell asleep, she sliced a few strands, he lost all of his strength, and the Philistines came in and captured him.

Samson had all of the power in the world. He was the strongest human alive and won battle after battle. He knew that his abilities didn't come from him but from God. He could have remained supernaturally strong for the rest of his days if he had just done what God asked him to do. We are like Samson, we have a supernatural power, and that is prayer. We get to tap into something that comes from far above us. Instead, we willingly cut our own hair. We decide that we can handle it all on our own. We don't need God's help. Why do we sabotage ourselves in the same way Samson did? We willingly give up our greatest power. We are insufficient to handle our problems on our own, but there is one who is greater than anything that we could possibly face. We don't receive because we don't ask. Ask you father for whatever it is that you need; he has promised to give it to you.

This does lead us into a bit of a difficult conversation. Why is it that God will just flat out not answer prayers? The quick answer is often something to do with those praying not believing or asking for the wrong thing. I think that it is more complicated than that, and I'm not sure that I have the answer. Let me give you an example: In 2017, Hurricane Maria was making her way through the Caribbean and was on track to hammer southern Florida. This was a category five storm with the capability to kill thousands and cause billions in damage. At the last minute, the hurricane changed her course. She went completely by southern Florida and created minimal issues for those living there. All over social media, you saw things about God having answered their prayers. Clearly, he must have in order for the hurricane to take an unexpected turn and leave the people safe. All was well, and God got the glory.

Now, let's take a trip 1,031 miles southeast to the island territory of Puerto Rico, more specifically, their capitol of San Juan. You see, Maria did not miss that city. In fact, she parked right on top of them for more than thirty hours. The wind and rain caused over ninety-one billion dollars of damage and killed over 3,000 people who had nowhere in which they could run. As image after image came in of the aftermath, my heart broke for the people. I also thought about how everyone was praising God for saving Florida. A question came to my mind that I didn't much know what to do with, "Did the people of Puerto Rico not pray?" Of course, they did. That's not what I was questioning. What I didn't understand was why their prayers were not answered.

We all have unanswered prayers in our lives. I prayed incessantly that God would heal my marriage. Obviously, that never happened. I don't know why. I like to look for the silver linings in every situation. My divorce did cause me to grow much closer to God than I have ever been. There's nothing that makes you cling to your faith quite like it being the only thing that you have left. This book would have never happened if my divorce would have never happened. I don't think that God ordained or wanted my marriage to fail, but I believe that God orchestrates beauty out of our messes. He will use the worst of situations to create in us something new and better. Quite frankly, sometimes life happens. It doesn't take God by surprise, but he allows it to happen. If he were to prevent every bad thing from ever happening, then we would have a weak faith because faith grows through adversity. Honestly, if he eliminated all evil from the world, you and I would cease to exist. I'm sure that we all have been the catalyst for hurting others before. Actually, as I recall, he did that one time with a flood. All of that is to say, I don't know why bad things happen to good people and good things happen to bad people. There is no explanation given in Matthew 5:45, " . . . For he makes his sun rise on the evil and on the good, and sends rain on the just and on the unjust." It simply is life. Crap will hit the fan, and devastation will always be a part of it. It was not only mankind that fell when Adam and Eve ate the forbidden fruit but all of creation as well. There will be pain and suffering until Christ returns. More prayers will go seemingly unanswered than we would like. Understand, that does not negate God's love for you. We will never fully understand why things will fall apart around us, but watch what God will do when he picks the pieces up and puts it all back together.

One of the best things to do whenever you are questioning why God hasn't answered your prayers or, at least, not in the way that you wanted is to remember prayers that he has answered. We all have had a myriad of prayers answered in our lives, some bigger than others. Store those away deep in the vaults of your mind, so that you can bring them out whenever you are struggling to understand. I think about times when I was flat broke, and not in the "I barely have enough to get by this month" way. There have been times throughout my life when my bank account read $0, and the paycheck was still a week or more away (take note if you want to pursue full-time ministry). Multiple times, a check seemingly randomly showed up in my mailbox. I have had occasions of finding money in my car that I have no idea how it got there. Those are moments that I go back to whenever I question if he's going to take care of me.

On top of that, there is one answered prayer that trumps all of them. My dad had a passive (at best) relationship with church and Christianity when I was growing up. He certainly wasn't against it, just not overly interested in it. I, on the other hand, was and am very involved in church. This started during my teenage years. He would show up whenever I was doing something at the church and on some holidays. I prayed for years that my dad would meet my heavenly father. Nothing. I didn't get the results that I wanted, but the prayers continued. After a few years, I didn't want to give up, but I was starting to lose heart. In my late teenage years, a guy that my dad had known earlier in life moved into town to start a church. After a while, my dad (I'm assuming at the behest of my stepmom) decided to check the church out. My hope started to grow again.

My dad eventually started to get pretty heavily involved in the church, so I decided to call the pastor, with whom I had a good relationship, and talk to him about my dad. This was my sophomore year in college, which was around six or seven years after I started praying for this. The pastor answered his phone, and after some small talk, I said, "I know that my dad has been coming to your church for a while and is getting more involved. I just wanted you to know that he hasn't really gone to church much." I continued, "I've tried to get him interested, but I don't think that I am the one to have an impact on him. I do think that you can be." There was a brief pause at the end of my sentence. Then he replied, "Funny that you should call me today, Kyle. We had our men's group meeting yesterday, and your dad came by early to help." This didn't surprise me one bit. My dad has always been a hard worker and never hesitates to lend a helping hand. Then, the pastor said, "We were alone, so I asked him why he decided to start coming to the church." The next words that he spoke floored me and warmed my heart all at once. "Your dad looked at me and said, 'I have seen what God has done in Kyle's life, and I decided to see what he could do in mine.' You have had a bigger impact than you know." I don't know exactly what we will feel when we're in heaven, but I imagine it will be an eternity of what I felt in that moment. Since then, my dad has been faithfully serving both the Lord and his church. My prayers were answered. Not when I wanted or how I thought they might be, but exactly as God had intended. Keep praying and never lose heart because he's listening.

My final word on prayer is this: we will always make time for what is most important to us. We have all thought, many times, that there are simply not enough hours in the day. There is a famous story about the great reformer, Martin Luther. He had become known for waking up early and spending four hours each morning in prayer. One day, someone asked him, "With all that you have going on, how do you find all that time to pray?" His response was, "With all that I have going on, how can I not find that time to pray?" Prayer was of the utmost importance to Luther, so he always made the time for it. He didn't believe that he could face the tasks of the day without asking God to empower him to do so. He made time to pray.

Nowadays, we are all just so busy. I'm a single guy with no kids, and I feel that I'm often scrambling to get accomplished all that I need to do each day. But, in reality, if you look at my life, you will see that I make plenty of time for things that are nonessential to my survival. Every day, I make time to work out, watch TV, check social media, play with my pets, talk to friends and family, read, etc. None of those things are inherently bad. I do find those things to be important in my life (some more so than others). I will even change my schedule around to accommodate those things because they bring me joy. What if we all found the same joy in spending time alone with God? Jesus made a regular practice of this.

Time after time, especially preceding or following some major event, Jesus got away from it all and was simply present with God. We don't know much about what he did in those times, besides the brief glimpse that we see in the garden of Gethsemane. I don't think his methodology is particularly as important as his intentionality, though. You may find a lot of other books that will explain to you what to do in those times that you spend alone with God. This one will not. My only advice is to simply be with him and let everything else flow from that. Some people will do nothing but pray, some read scripture or other books, some listen to music, some dance, some sing, some cry; there is no one size fits all answer to what will bring your heart in line with that of the Father's. Heck, I've always said that one of the best spiritual practices is to take a nap. We are all unique, and God will meet us where we are. He knows what causes the spark of our spiritual fire, and he'll pour gasoline on it. The important thing is just that you are with him.

To bring this chapter full circle, it was nothing that I did with my dad on our day together that made it so meaningful. It was simply that I had spent the time with him— just my dad and me.

Go, spend time with your divine father. Feel his love and compassion. Let him tell you how delighted he is to be with you. Meet his gaze as he stares at you and smiles. You are his child, beloved and cherished. Take the time, enter into the throne room, crawl into his royal lap, and just be with him for a while. If you do that regularly, you will never be the same.

6

The Man at the Well

ONE OF THE MOST important things that we can do to establish a better relationship with God is to get to know more about how he loves us. That is simply how you deepen any relationship; you learn more about who the other person is. Since God already knows all that there is to know about us, we are a little behind in that department. How is it that we can begin to know the characteristics of our heavenly father? While we can go to him in prayer, it is not often that he speaks to us in a loud, audible voice, so a question-and-answer session is not likely. Jesus actually addressed this in John 15:9, "As the Father has loved me, so have I loved you. Abide in my love." Every bit of God's love is revealed to us by how Jesus loves us and loved those whom he was around during his earthly ministry. If we want to know "How great a love the Father has given us," (1 John 3:1, HCSB) we must look at how great a love that Jesus had for those around him.

I have chosen one of my favorite stories in all of scripture to show the character of Jesus— as well as God. This story involves an encounter between Jesus and someone who is seen as *less than*. Actually, the person whom Jesus encountered would be seen as ceremonially unclean. Let me break down what that means. In the Old Testament, the first five books are known as "the Law." Most of the Jewish laws come from the books of Exodus, Deuteronomy, and Leviticus, with some other rules being thrown in here and there throughout the entirety of the Jewish canon. Following the Law was *the* most important thing for the Israelites. Their relationship with God, at least how they saw it, was that they glorified him and earned his favor by following the rules. If you followed the rules, then you were considered clean. Along the way, the religious leaders added hundreds of other laws that were not in scripture and thus made upholding the Law nearly impossible. There were 613 laws in all, to be exact. If you failed with a single law, then you failed the entire law. This would make you ceremonially unclean, and those who were unclean could not even enter the Temple Mount to worship God until they went through a proper cleansing ritual. Being "clean" mattered more than anything else for the Jews.

This event comes from John 4. Jesus and his disciples were heading back to Galilee from Jerusalem, mainly as a way to avoid an unneeded conflict with the Pharisees. He would have plenty of needed ones in the future. In all likelihood, they were on their way to Capernaum and Peter's house, where Jesus crashed when he wasn't needed elsewhere. This trip was around seventy miles, which they would make on foot. This would equate to a four or five-day trip. There was a slight issue, though. Right smack dab in the path from Jerusalem to Capernaum was a place called Samaria. As it turns out, the Jews and Samaritans hated each other and not just a little bit. The Jews believed that the Samaritans were the scum of the earth and lesser than stray dogs. The Samaritans didn't much appreciate being treated as such, so they returned the sentiment equally.

The reason why the Jews looked down upon the Samaritans so much was because the Samaritans had defiled their Jewish blood and lineage. In 721 BC, the Assyrians besieged the then capital of Israel, Samaria. Once the invading army prevailed, they took all of the citizens captive. With the Jews now out of Samaria, gentiles (non-Jewish people) moved in. Eventually, the Samaritans moved back home and lived amongst and intermarried with the gentiles living there. This led the other Jews to view them as traitorous and sinners. So, generational racism and hatred became the foundation of how they would relate to one another.

This hatred was so deep that the "good" Jews would avoid walking through Samaria. They believed that even getting dirt on their sandals from the Samaritan land would make them unclean. Instead of taking the quickest and most direct path through the despised region, they would walk around it. This would add on another day to their trek. Imagine hating someone so much that you would be willing to greatly inconvenience yourself just to avoid them. Well, maybe we don't have to try too hard to imagine that.

Jesus decided that he was going to walk straight through Samaria. I don't believe that his motivation was that he wanted to take the simplest, shortest route. No, Jesus had other intentions for going this way. There was someone in need of meeting him, and Jesus never misses a meeting. Simply by going through Samaria, Jesus, who was seen as a rabbi, risked his social and religious reputation. This was truly a scandalous event. Many would have decided that upholding their public persona would have been of more importance than whatever could happen in that forsaken land. I don't believe there was even a choice for Jesus. He knew where he was needed and did not care about the social norms that said that he should not go there. Jesus is always willing to go where others dare not tread.

Tired from their journey, Jesus and the disciples stopped at a well to take a little break. The twelve then went into the town to buy food. While they may have been hungry, the ultimate reason that they were sent away was because the Savior needed to have a private moment with an unexpecting companion. She had a divine meeting scheduled as well; she just didn't know it yet. John 4:6 tells us that, "It was about the sixth hour," when the woman showed up. That meant that it was noon. It is safe to assume that no details are ever thrown into the Bible frivolously. This fact actually reveals much about the one coming to draw water. Imagine being in the Middle East and how hot it gets there. Then, I want you to think about when the best time would be to go and get your daily supply of water. It certainly would not be at noon, when it would be miserably hot from the inescapable sun. That, however, is when we see this woman arrive. Why would she come then? I can think of only one reason. She wanted to come at a time when no one else would be there. Her goal was simply to avoid the crowd. We will find out the reason for that soon, but it is obvious that this woman was an outcast.

As this societal scoundrel reached the well, she realized, certainly to her dismay, that there was someone else there. Quickly, she recognized that this wasn't just anybody, but it was a Jewish man. This had to be her worst nightmare. Not only was this her cultural enemy, but men were infinitely more powerful in society at that time. This situation had a very, very good chance of going poorly for our pariah. Something quite odd happened next; Jesus asked her for a drink of water. He didn't demand or command but simply asked. That may not seem like a crazy gesture to us, but in the woman's mind, this was something spectacular. By asking, Jesus gave her the right to refuse. He gave her power that she had not felt in an extremely long time, maybe ever. Jesus' first words to the woman were those of kindness. He was just setting the stage for his love to put on quite the show.

The woman was taken aback by the Divine asking for a drink. John 4:9 reads, "How is it that you, a Jew, ask for a drink from me, a woman of Samaria?" Never be fooled into thinking that this woman didn't know her station in life. She understood who she was and where she ranked. She knew that she was out of her depth in this conversation. She may even have thought that this stranger had ulterior motives. Jesus, as he often did, began to speak in the spiritual metaphorical. He told her that if she knew who he was, then she'd ask him for a drink of the "living water" (John 4:10). What played out from there is a classic case of miscommunication. Society at that time took words very literally. You said what you meant, and you meant what you said. The Messiah was constantly running into issues whenever he would speak such ways because the people simply did not understand (think about Nicodemus being told that he needed to be born again in John 3:7). This Samaritan was no different. Regardless, Jesus had her attention.

There was one issue that she brought up, though. Jesus didn't even have a bucket to draw any water from the well. How in the world was he going to give her any water? Furthermore, she informed him that the well once belonged to Jacob, and certainly this seemingly-random-Jewish man could not be greater than the biblical patriarch. Surprisingly, Christ left this question unanswered. He continued on to say, "but whoever drinks of the water that I will give him will never be thirsty again" (John 4:14). I can only imagine how wide the woman's eyes got upon hearing this. The idea of never again having to make the arduous hike in the middle of the day must have intrigued her. I wonder if she even heard the rest of that verse, "The water that I will give to him will become in him a spring of water welling up to eternal life." He was offering her salvation, but she could not see the spiritual because she was so focused on her current circumstance. That is a place in which many of us receive our mail. Fully committed to the idea of making her life easier, she blurted out in John 4:15, "Sir, give me this water, so that I will not be thirsty or have to come here to draw water." She had missed the point, but Jesus was not ready to give up on her.

Jesus told her to go get her husband, and she informed him that she didn't actually have one of those. Then, the next statement that the man at the well spoke must have rocked this woman's world. "You are right in saying that, 'I have no husband'; for you have had five husbands, and the one you have now is not your husband" (John 4:17–18). We have now found out why the woman was coming to the well at noon and the reason she avoided the crowd. There is no certainty as to why she has had five previous husbands. Did they all die? Did every marriage end in divorce? Some combination of the two? By the way that she wanted to bypass the crowd at the well, it stands to reason that divorce was the likely culprit behind the brokenness. On top of that, it seems as though she was living with a man who was not her husband. A side note on divorce at that time: women could not ask for them, only men. They did not need to have a reason— just a desire to do so. Jesus addressed this in Matthew 19. This woman, in all likelihood, had been tossed aside unfairly by five different men. It is no wonder that she wasn't interested in getting married a sixth time. With this information, we have now peeled back another layer as to who this woman was and the scarlet letter displayed upon her chest.

I do not feel as though I am an expert in much, but I have a great understanding of the emotions one will feel as they go through a divorce. I know the impact it has on self-image and self-esteem. I think that I am qualified to offer some insights into how this wounded woman was feeling about herself. Admittedly, when I used to read John 4, I would treat the woman as though she was *less than*. I thought that it must have been her mistakes that played the greatest role in her situation. Oh, how life has a way of teaching us things that all the books in the world could not convey to our hearts. I have learned how it feels to have someone who has chosen to love you to decide that they are finished with that task. Every part of the Samaritan woman was broken. Her mental state, self-esteem, self-image, value, and spirituality were marred by the phrase "not enough." That was the only way in which she saw herself. Even when she slowly pulled herself out of the pit of despair, those words would have never left her mind. With each failed relationship and marriage, that sinister thought gained more and more credence. She could not see herself for who she was, only for who she was not. Her heart had been ravished and torn to pieces. There was very little left to salvage. At best, she may have thought of herself as a reclamation project. Deep down though, she knew that she could never be fixed. Her hope was that she would go through each day being unseen. Her truest desire was to dissipate into nothingness, so that she would become what her heart felt. I know that this is what she felt because it is what I felt, and she went through it five times. She could not possibly have seen herself as a child of God. Her pain had swept away that notion and replaced it with the idea that no one would want her. I no longer read this story as though she was deserving of her situation. I now read this story as though I am looking in a mirror. Rather, I should say that is how I read the story after my divorce until, much like this shattered Samaritan, God showed me that he had much more in store for me.

Upon hearing the intimate details about her life, the woman knew that she was not talking to just any man. She exclaims, "Sir, I perceive that you are a prophet." That is John 4:19. [I ask that you allow me to take us down a totally unrelated path for just a moment. I have a friend that was engaged to be married. His fiancé thought it would be a great idea to send all of the pictures that they had taken together to be made into a book. On the front cover of the book, she had them put their relationship verse, which was 1 John 4:19. That line reads, "We love because he first loved us." Cute. Along the way, some wires got crossed, and it instead read John 4:19, which says, "The woman said to him, 'Sir, I perceive that you are a prophet.'" My friend quite enjoyed that line and did not allow his fiancé to send it back to be fixed. Back to the important stuff.] Jesus went on to reveal to her that worshipping God would no longer be about a building (the Samaritans had their own temple in which they performed sacrifices and rituals), but instead about true, spiritual relationship with God. The wheels in the woman's head started spinning. She told Christ that she knew that the, "Messiah is coming" (John 4:25), and that he would explain all of that to them. To this, Jesus revealed to the least likely of all people that he is indeed the Messiah.

This would have bucked all conventional wisdom. Everything about whom he revealed himself to makes no sense. She was a woman, and thus her testimony meant nothing in society at that time. She was an outcast, and no one would have cared what she had to say. She had been divorced five times and was in an unholy relationship. She was a Samaritan, and the Jews thought they were of no value. She was a sinful nobody. Why did Jesus choose her? Because she was not a nobody to him, but a cherished child of God. She is whom he came to this world to save. After all, Jesus said, "Those who are well have no need of a physician, but those who are sick. I came not to call the righteous, but sinners" (Mark 2:17).

As I stated at the beginning of this chapter, this was a scandalous event, perhaps the most scandalous in all of scripture. Jesus went into a place in which Jews would not want to be caught dead— literally. He found a divorced Samaritan woman and had a conversation with her. Not only did Jews not converse with Samaritans, but rabbis (a title in which Jesus was given) did not talk freely to any women in public. Her own people had rejected her, yet there she was, with the one who had created her. Every aspect of this encounter could have cost Jesus his reputation and his status. He simply did not care. He was willing to go where no one else would, to reach someone no one else would, and love her like no one else would. That is who Jesus is, and that is who the Father is. No one resides outside the grasp of divine affection— nobody.

The story did not end there. What happened next is truly astounding. After Jesus revealed his true identity to her, she headed back into town and began telling everyone about this man that she had met. This is remarkable. Remember why she was out at the well at noon? It was so she could avoid seeing the people of her town. She wanted nothing to do with them because they wanted nothing to do with her. Now, she laid aside all the discomfort that she had felt around them. She was a changed woman because she had encountered one who loved her and treated her kindly. Because of this woman, the whole town went to meet Jesus. One of the most extraordinary lines in all of scripture is the one that concludes this story. After having encountered Jesus for themselves, the townsfolk said to the sinner turned evangelist, "It is no longer because of what you said that we believe, for we have heard for ourselves, and we know that this is indeed the Savior of the world" (John 4:42). An entire town was welcomed into eternity because the woman at the well could not stay quiet about the man at the well.

Jesus saw something in her that she did not see in herself. She was so caught up in her sinfulness that she lost sight of the fact that she was a child of God. It wasn't until the heathen met the Healer that everything changed for her. Jesus loved her at that exact moment for exactly who she was. There was no stipulation for her to receive his love. All that she had to do was spend but a moment with him. Because of that moment, lives were changed forever. Not only hers, but the whole town's as well. If we logically think through this for a second, then we will arrive at the conclusion that those people of Sychar (the village in which this took place), who had just met the Savior, would have gone on to tell their friends, family, and children. The name of Jesus would have been preached and talked about in those parts for generations to come. This all happened because of the woman. Jesus took the lowest of all people and turned her into a missionary. She could not have dreamt of such a thing, but Jesus saw a better future for her. He saw one where she would forever be in relationship with him. She no longer needed to go from man to man because she had found the Son of Man. No longer would she have to try to avoid the withering stare of a judgmental society because she was seen by her creator. Her heart no longer lacked for love because it was now filled by the Holy Spirit. Jesus went out of his way to meet someone who was a nobody, so that he could love her and create for her a better future. This is the same way that Jesus treats us, which means that this is the same way that the Father treats us.

You see, we are all that Samaritan woman. We all have a past of which we are not proud. We allow those sins and mistakes to define who we are. That's when the doubt sinks into our minds. Instead of hearing the gentle whisper of our father telling us that we are loved and that we matter to him, we hear, "You're not good enough!" The worst part is that we are all ready to believe that lie. That clever serpent slithers down to us and asks, "Did God really say that? Did he really say that he loves you? What about all the times that you've failed? Sinner!" We must completely change our mindset. This isn't easy. The world constantly tells us that we are not enough. When we meet eyes with the judgmental person in the mirror, he or she tells us that we are *less than* and a nobody. We have been trained to feel like garbage and to think that we are garbage. I am here to argue the other side. The side that says that Jesus has called you his, and that he will not lose one of his prized possessions. There is an old adage that we do not know the origins of, but gets attributed to Mark Twain, "It's easier to fool people than it is to convince them that they have been fooled." We all play the fool regularly. We have been fooled into believing that we are a lost cause and yesterday's news. We believe that, because we are not perfect and not worthy, God cannot possibly be head over heels for us. So, we begin to work ourselves to death to try to earn that love. All that leads to is us hitting the bed every night with calloused hands, tired feet, and empty hearts.

What did the Samaritan woman do to earn Jesus' love and kindness? Nothing, aside from being desperately in need of it. She was simply going about her day, living in the boring and mundane. Then, she had an encounter with the one who loved her the most and everything changed. Her soul was invaded by the great Conqueror. Jesus met her where she was, not only physically but spiritually, and provided her with all that she would need— himself. There was no judgment in his words, nor did he utter one syllable of condemnation. According to the world, this woman was filth. According to Jesus, she was a treasure. This is how Jesus related to all the harlots and heathens that he met. It was only the self-righteous with whom he had any issues.

Are you desperately in need of the love and kindness that Jesus offers? He wants to give it to you in droves. He has no intention of holding back. All that you have to do is go to him. It doesn't need to be anything spectacular. Jesus is always willing to meet you right where you are. Wherever it is that you are reading this book, Jesus is there waiting for you. You need not bring anything but yourself, that's the only thing that interests him. Just like our broken trollop found out two thousand years ago, there is a man at the well, and he is the Savior of the world. Will you go and sit with him for a while? Let him tell you everything that you've ever done, and then hear him say that he loves you and so does the Father. That man will always be at the well, waiting to have his divine meeting with you, ready to give you a drink, and to fill you with the love and kindness that you so desperately need.

7

There Was Jesus

I WOULD LIKE TO pause here and address something of pertinence. This book has been written under the guise that God is our heavenly father. I have used examples of my own dad as a way to look at how God interacts with us. Some of you reading this cannot relate to those stories because you do not come from a solid, healthy familial background. I did not grow up in the classic idea of a nuclear family, but I did grow up in a family that loved me (and, to my knowledge, still do). Although I lost out on my mom, dad, brother, and sister living together for all of my life, I gained a stepmom and stepdad that took care of me, raised me, and regularly showed their affection to me and my siblings. I am one of the lucky ones. Far too many people grow up in broken families. Too many children have the hurt of an absentee parent in their lives. The most common emotion that some people feel towards a parent is disappointment. Sadly, abuse from a parent is not foreign in this country, whether it be sexual, physical, mental, or psychological. This breaking of the covenant of love that should exist between a parent and his or her child will linger well beyond when the action(s) took place. We live in a broken world, where travesty becomes a commonality amongst family members. While I have not experienced any such things in my life, I am not naïve. I know that this happens far more than we would ever want to know. I have heard many, many heart-breaking stories over the years. All of that is to say that not everyone gets a warm and fuzzy feeling whenever they read the word *father*, and I want to be sensitive to and acknowledge that. For those of you who have experienced a father who failed to fulfill his role, I am truly sorry.

There is a story in the Gospel of John (which I imagine you are well aware by now that I really enjoy that book) where parents failed to be there for and stand up for their child. This account takes place across the entirety of chapter 9. Jesus had just had a lovely encounter with the Jewish leaders in which he pronounced that, "Before Abraham was, I am" (John 8:58). The importance of that statement is twofold. One, he was stating that he existed before Abraham, who lived about 2000 years before Jesus' incarnation. Two, he blatantly called himself God by giving himself the same name in which God gave to himself when talking to Moses in Exodus 3:14, "I Am." Obviously, the Jewish leaders didn't particularly appreciate such statements, so they picked up rocks and prepared to stone Jesus to death, but he got away. This all took place at the Temple.

After that event, Jesus and his twelve disciples were walking away from the previous scene when they saw a blind man. John made it a point to inform us that this man was born blind (John 9:1). Having a physical disability makes for a difficult life now, but it was even more so back then. If you couldn't work, then you had no way to earn money to eat. This meant that there were two ways in which you could survive— either your family took care of you or you begged. This man was a beggar. We do not know exactly how old this man was. Based on information that we will learn later in this chapter, he was considered an adult. He would have spent every day along the street, hoping that someone would either give him some money or food to eat. That was this man's entire life. It appears as though he was smart enough to park himself on a well-traveled road that led to the Temple, and thus would have had a parade of foot traffic pass him by every day.

Once the disciples saw the blind man, they had a question for Jesus, "Who sinned, this man or his parents, that he was born blind?" (John 9:2). There was a prevailing belief back in those times that if anyone had an ailment, disability, or was suffering in any way (see the book of Job), then it was because God was punishing someone for a sin. They even believed that children who were born disabled were the result of a parent's sin. Unfortunately, many still hold on to different versions of this teaching today. Seeing that they had God with them, the disciples figured they could get to the bottom of this man's case. Surprisingly, Jesus turned this entire notion on its head by informing them that his blindness had nothing to do with sin. Then, he told them that this man was going to be used to show the glory of God. Do you remember the part in the previous chapter of this book where I explained the importance of being "clean"? Those who had any sort of disability were considered to be perpetually unclean because of the belief that it was related to sin. This man had lived his whole life with the knowledge that he was not worthy of God's love, and there was not a single thing that he could possibly do about it. Yet, here is the Light of the World telling his disciples that God's glory would shine through this blind man.

One of the most interesting things about Jesus is that he seemed to have a myriad of ways to perform miracles. There was no one-size-fits-all approach. Sometimes, he touched someone; sometimes, he just spoke; one time, he stuck his fingers in a dude's ears; and this time, he made some mud and rubbed it in the man's eyes. No one seems to be sure as to why he did it this way, but I'm sure that he had a reason. In fact, the healing was not actually completed at that moment. The Great Physician sent the man to the nearby Pool of Siloam to wash the mud out of his eyes. I have to wonder what the man was thinking as he made the walk to the pool. Maybe he was hopeful, or maybe he thought Jesus was crazy. Either way, he had mud in his eyes that needed washed out, so to the pool he went. After washing off the mud, the man opened his eyes and saw for the first time. Maybe that is why Jesus did the miracle this way. The word Siloam means "sent" (John 9:7).

Perhaps Jesus was showing that he was "sent" to open the eyes of the blind, just as Isaiah 35:5 prophesied that the coming Messiah would do. Jesus very well may have been announcing, in his own way, that he was the promised Savior to this man.

Once the man's eyes were opened and he took in the beauty of this world for the first time, he decided that he needed to go home and let everyone know. Excited as anyone could possibly be, he arrived home and was immediately met with skepticism. His neighbors and friends began to question if it was really him. Naturally, an argument broke out. Some believed that he was who he said he was, while others didn't. Some thought that he was someone else who looked like their blind buddy pretending to be him. Imagine how that must have felt for the now-not-blind man. He would have been on an emotional, spiritual, and physical high, only to be forced to come crashing down. Rather than rejoicing and celebrating with him, they were debating his identity. All the while, he kept exclaiming, "I am the man" (John 9:9).

The deliberation continued. The crowd wanted to know how it was that he was suddenly able to see. Undeniably, that was a very fair question. If someone whom you had known for years was blind was no longer blind, then a few follow-up questions would be in order. He explained to them what had happened with Jesus, the mud, and the Pool of Siloam. "Where is he (Jesus)?" the people asked (John 9:12). Suddenly it occurred to the seeing man that, in all of his excitement, he never went back to Jesus. So, he informed them that he was not sure where Jesus was. Rather than throw a party for the miracle that had just occurred, the neighbors and friends decided to take the man to the Pharisees. How's that for the rug being pulled out from under his feet? This should have been the happiest day of his life, but now he was being dragged in front of the religious leaders who had told him his entire life that he was nothing more than a sinner. Just a little reminder, this was fresh off the heels of the Pharisees trying to murder Jesus. I think that you can imagine how this played out with them.

Once he was forced to be in front of the self-deemed spiritually superior, we find out a very important piece of information:

this miracle took place on the Sabbath. Just like today, the Sabbath occurred every week, starting at sundown on Friday and lasting until sundown on Saturday. God created the Sabbath to give people a day of rest after a busy week. The Jews took (and still take) the Sabbath extremely seriously. Do you remember how I mentioned in the previous chapter that the Jewish leaders added hundreds of more rules to the Law than what scripture stated? Well, most of them pertained to what you could and, more importantly, could not do on the Sabbath. You could not do any work. You could only take so many steps. You could not cook, clean, or run errands. I will give you an example that I witnessed personally whilst I visited Israel back in 2017. In the hotel, they had an elevator that was set to automatically stop at each floor. They did this because they considered pressing the button to call the elevator "work", and the stairs were certainly not an option. Nothing, and I mean nothing, was to happen on the Sabbath except for rest. Of course, Jesus regularly administered miracles on these most holy of days. It was one of the biggest contentions that the religious leaders had with him. They had already tried to kill Jesus, so this was only going to enrage them all the more.

The man who had his eyes opened was questioned by the Pharisees, and he explained to them exactly what had happened. This caused a conundrum for our pompous group of ruling men. Some said that Jesus was a sinner because he was doing "work" on the Sabbath. Others were saying that a sinner could not have healed a blind man. They were divided amongst themselves, as John explains in verse 16. It is not like they could deny the miracle had happened; the proof was standing right in front of them. They probably walked by him almost every day as they went to the Temple. Many of them may have even given him some money or food. They decided to ask the beggar what he thought about Jesus. He told them that he believed that the man who healed him was, "a prophet" (John 9:17). This was not what they wanted to hear. Although, I don't know what they were expecting him to have said. How could he possibly have said anything negative about the man who had completely changed his life? Nevertheless, the Pharisees did not like what he had to say. They began to question whether or not this man was telling the truth. That was when they decided to send for his parents.

This will lead us into what I believe is one of the most heart-breaking scenes in all of the Bible. It should have been good news that his parents were about to show up. Parents should always rush to their child's side to protect them. Unfortunately, as far too many people have experienced in their lives, parents are not always what parents should be.

The parents of the man who was on trial were summoned and questioned. They were asked a couple of fairly straightforward questions in verse 19, "Is this your son, who you say was born blind? How then does he now see?" They affirmed to the oppressive rulers that the man was indeed their son, but they did not know how it was that he had gained his sight. Everything that they said was true. This is the first mention of the parents in this narrative, but it does seem, based on verse 22, that they were aware of what had happened. This should have been one of the most joyous days of their lives. Parents should always hope for and work for the best for their children. Sadly, other motivations sometimes override a parent's sensibilities, and that was the case here. Instead of standing up for their son, they gave him over to cruel men who were wanting nothing but to punish him for being the recipient of God's grace. They told the religious leaders, "He is of age. He will speak for himself" (John 9:21). Verse 22 explains to us why the parents threw their own offspring under the bus, "His parents said these things because they feared the Jews (meaning Jewish leaders), for the Jews had already agreed that if anyone should confess Jesus to be Christ, he was to be put out of the synagogue." They were afraid for their own well-being. If they were kicked out of the synagogue, that would mean they would no longer be able to participate in the rituals that were required of them. As far as they knew, this would disqualify them from spending eternity in heaven. What were they to do in that situation, sacrifice their souls or their son? They chose to leave their son to stand on his own and be at the mercy of men who did not make a habit of offering it.

For a second time, the Pharisees brought the innocent man to be questioned. They made their thoughts on Jesus known by telling the man that Jesus was a sinner. Something that I have always found fascinating about this chapter is that everyone except for the recipient of the miracle seems to know who performed it. The parents knew not to mention Jesus' name, and the Pharisees were all worked up because they knew who it was that was working miracles all over Israel. This speaks directly to their heart. Everything that Jesus did pointed to him being the Messiah, but they refused to accept it because it would ruin their status of being the religious rulers of Israel. Those who considered themselves amongst the elite did not do so with the intention of ever losing that lofty status. Some things never change. In fact, when the Pharisees accused Jesus of being a sinner to the man who could now see, they told him to give glory to God instead (John 9:24). Sometimes, irony is a beautiful thing.

The back and forth that then took place between the man and the Pharisees was truly wonderful, until it turned tragic. The man responded to the leaders with simple facts, "Whether he is a sinner I do not know. One thing I do know, that though I was blind, now I see" (John 9:25). From the minute that Jesus took on flesh until forevermore, no one who has been impacted by him can deny his work. The man knew that his entire life had been defined by one thing— he was blind. That was true for each and every day. That morning, when he woke up, was no different. He may have felt the warmth of the sun and listened to the chirping of the birds, but he did not see them. He may have smelled the bread baking and heard people laughing, but he did not see them. Suddenly, a man came into his life and changed everything, but even still, he did not see him. All that he knew was that he had been blind, but now, he was able to see. There was no argument against that. Jesus' work in our lives is always profound and miraculous, even when we do not see it right away.

The Pharisees again asked the man to recount his story. At this point, the healed man was confused. "I have told you already, and you would not listen. Why do you want to hear it again? Do you also want to be his disciples?" (John 9:27). I believe that this was asked in total innocence. Nobody would dare talk to the Pharisees like that, especially in public. Well, nobody except Jesus. Publicly clashing with the religious rulers could cost you your freedom, life, and salvation. Highly offended at this audacious statement, the Pharisees lashed out at the man. They insulted him and informed him of just how holy they were. They finished their little tirade by saying that they didn't even know where Jesus had come from. Unexpectedly, the man who had been blind was emboldened to speak his mind. As it turns out, he happened to be a little bit wiser and more knowledgeable than anyone could have expected. He crafted an airtight, inarguable, theological statement that put the tyrannical teachers to shame.

> Why, this is an amazing thing! You do not know where he comes from, and yet he opened my eyes. We know that God does not listen to sinners, but if anyone is a worshiper of God and does his will, God listens to him. Never since the world began has it been heard that anyone opened the eyes of a man born blind. If this man were not from God, he could do nothing (John 9:30–33).

Perfection! Every word that he said was in line with everything that was believed at the time. By their own logic and what they taught, the Pharisees were now backed into a corner. They could not have possibly argued that someone who healed the blind, an act that was only to be accomplished by the coming savior, could have been a sinner. With nowhere left to go, the supposed men of God hurled more insults at their newfound adversary and kicked him out of the synagogue.

Take a moment and think about how this guy's day had gone. He was sitting alone along the street, as he did every day, minding his own business when Jesus and the disciples happened to walk by him. He never even asked to be healed, but Jesus decided to open his eyes anyways. He made his way to the pool of Siloam and washed away the mud. Amazingly, for the first time, he could see. He rushed home to celebrate with friends and family, only to be met with skepticism. He then was forced to stand in front of the religious leaders who verbally abused him and made an example out of him. Even his own parents failed to stand by his side. He had not asked for any of this. When he woke up, he imagined that it would just be a normal day. He didn't have much of a life, but he had his life. Now, he had nothing. Everyone had turned against him. I imagine that if you asked him at that moment, he would have said that he wished he would have never met Jesus. He would have much rather still been beside the road, begging and blind. Sadly, the thing that he had seen the most since his eyes were opened was darkness.

With nowhere to go and no one left to support him, the disappointed man began to walk down the road, perhaps back to the place where he spent his days begging. That, however, is not how his story ends. Having heard the news, Jesus sought to find the man. When he finally reached him, he asked him, "Do you believe in the Son of Man?" (John 9:35). This was a familiar voice for the man to hear. He must have known instantly who it was that was talking to him. For the first time, his eyes were able to look upon the one who created them and healed them. "'And who is he, sir, that I may believe in him?' Jesus said to him, 'You have seen him, and it is he who is speaking to you'" (John 9:36–37). After seeing nothing but pain since sight had been given to him, he was able to see the Great Healer. The man put his faith in Christ that day and is spending his eternity by his side at this very moment.

The most spectacular thing that happened in this passage was not the miracle. It wasn't the trial that took place, nor the man giving his life to Christ. It was that when there was no one else that would stand by this man, *there was Jesus.* The man would never have to walk alone again because his Savior promised to walk alongside him for all eternity. Everyone that this man had met in his life viewed him in one way: blind. His parents, his family, his friends, his neighbors, the Pharisees, those who passed him by on the street, and even the disciples. Jesus saw him differently. He was not just some poor guy who was being punished because of sin. No, Jesus saw him for who he truly was, a child of God who was created in the likeness of the Father. Then, when he was left with nothing, Jesus sought him out and called him a name that he had never could have imagined— *mine*.

That is the name Jesus offers to all of us. We are all given the opportunity to become his. The same question that he asked that man nearly two thousand years ago is the same one that he asks us today, "Do you believe?"

Some in this world can really relate to the man who began John 9 being addressed simply as, "a man blind from birth" (John 9:1). Something has happened that makes you think that you are *less than*. You believe that you are defined by your deficiency and mistakes, and that's it. You have had people turn their backs on you time after time. Loved ones did not treat you in the way in which you deserved to be treated. You have been put down and insulted your whole life. Your eyes have seen far more darkness than light in this beautiful, cruel world. Religious leaders have accomplished nothing but to instill fear and condemnation in your life. You have been used and looked down upon by everyone. Maybe you're in a position in which you have no one and nowhere to go. Maybe you, too, have been completely let down by your parents. Instead of standing up for you, they threw you to wolves and let them devour you. Much like that blind man, you have just learned to deal with the disappointment and travesty that is your life. I have good news for you: your story is not over.

There is nothing that can change those hurts of your past. Ultimately, what is done is done. That does not mean that the glory of God is not going to shine through you. Just as the man who was restored was sought out by Jesus, he is seeking you today. He wants to come into your life and offer you a better now and future. He knows every bit of hurt that you are feeling. He knows that you think you are alone in this broken world. Jesus has heard the news that you are in need of a savior, and he has come alongside you. All that you need to do is respond in the same way as the seeing man and say, "I believe." If you do that, you will be just as changed as that man was. Yes, there will still be hurt, pain, and disappointment in this world. The man who was healed still had to deal with the fallout from his confrontation with the Pharisees. The promise is not that heartbreak and hard times will go away. The promise is that you will never have to face them alone. Maybe you cannot relate to my feel-good stories of loving parents, but you can know the love of your creator. If you do decide to allow Jesus to change your life, then you will be able look back throughout your story at what he has brought you through and say, "There was Jesus."

8

The Battle

WE HAVE SPENT THE entirety of this book discussing how God loves us. While that is absolutely true, we must also discuss the fact that we all have a problem as well. That problem is sin. This has been a problem since Adam and Eve were first deceived in the Garden. Whenever they went against God's desire for their lives, they created a ripple effect that is still being felt today. God's favorite creation was forever tainted from that moment on. This is the common thread that is woven throughout the entire Bible. This is also the answer as to why there is so much hurt and pain in this world. Everyone who has ever lived (besides Jesus) has two things in common: we are all created in God's image and sin causes us to rebel against our creator.

Merriam-Webster defines sin as a, "transgression of the law of God."[1] For the Jews, that was the hundreds of laws in which they had to follow. For the Christian, that is to not love God and love people as God desires of us. The word sin actually has an interesting history. At the time of the New Testament writing, it was an archery term. There was one goal whenever someone went out for target practice with a bow and arrow: to hit the bullseye.

1. Merriam-Webster, s.v. "sin," accessed February 5, 2021, http://www.merriam-webster.com/dictionary/sin.

Obviously, that was not easy. More often than not, people missed. Whenever they would miss, they *sinned*. If you missed the bullseye by three inches to the left, then you sinned three inches to the left. Sinning was simply missing the bullseye. That is what sin is in relation to God as well. We should always aim to hit the mark for how he wishes us to live our lives— as spelled out by scripture. Much like hitting the bullseye with an arrow, this is easier said than done. Heck, I'm lucky if my arrow even hits the target on most days.

Another thing about sin is that it requires consequences. If you remember when we talked about Adam and Eve in chapter 4, they faced punishment for their eating of the forbidden fruit. They were kicked out of the Garden of Eden, childbirth became painful, and people would forever have to work hard to survive. Most people do not like to talk about God as punitive. Admittedly, this is not my favorite way to talk about him either. There is a large part of me that wishes God allowed us to do what we wanted with no penalties. That is not how a good father would ever raise his children, though. As of this writing, I have not been blessed with children of my own, but I am an uncle to a slew of nieces and nephews. I have been around the raising of children, even if I was not the one raising them. Children need rules or they will greatly harm themselves. The number one priority of parents is basically to keep their kid alive. Kids like to battle against that for some reason. God's rules are not there to stifle us, but to protect us. That is why there must be consequences for our incessant need to rebel.

Once again, let me take you back in time to one of my first memories, although this one is a little foggy. This memory has been more formed by others recollecting it to me than me fully remembering it. I was probably around four years old at the time. It was a Sunday morning, and my mom had taken my sister to church. I'm not sure why she didn't take my brother and me with her. It was probably because we were a little too rambunctious for the rigidness of church, and she didn't feel like dealing with us that morning. Regardless, we were home with my dad. He worked the midnight shift as a police dispatcher at the time, so he was still in bed. My brother, two neighbor girls, and myself were playing in the yard. Somewhere along the way, someone decided that we should play in our storage building. I have no idea whose idea it was to start playing with matches, but that is exactly what we did. This would be a good time to remind you that my dad was the deputy chief of the volunteer fire department in our town at the time. Also, one of his main roles was to teach fire prevention. Life is full of irony.

Someone decided that it would be a fun idea to light the old recliner in the storage building on fire. You know where this is heading. Before we knew it, the recliner was fully ablaze, and everything else around was following suit. We all got out of the building in time, but the fire was consuming everything inside. It just so happened that I had left a little toy in there and went to go back in after it. Luckily, someone stopped me. My dad was awakened to find that there was a fire in his own backyard. He was forced to call the fire department to come put it out. He should receive some credit, though, for being the first firefighter to make it to the scene. To this day, my brother claims that it was the neighbor girls who had the terrible idea. All I know is that I was an innocent bystander to what happened. In case you're wondering, my toy was not saved. A tragic loss.

Naturally, punishment was in store for the both of us. I do not remember the full extent of the sentence, but I do recall that we were banned from going to the fire department for quite a while, which happened to be our favorite place to spend time. No one would question my parents for punishing us. We deserved it. We made dumb choices that could have had life-altering or even life-ending results. We needed to learn our lesson for what we had done. My parents didn't reprimand us because they hated us— quite the opposite, in fact. This is the same way in which sin works. If we are left to our own devices, we are all going to make dumb decisions that are only going to harm us. This is why there must be consequences for sin. It is most often through the consequences that we learn to avoid making such decisions. These reprimands happen out of God's love for us.

The first part of Romans 6:23 tells us that, "The wages of sin is death." This verse is speaking not only to a physical death that we will all experience someday but to a spiritual death as well. This death is an eternal separation from God in a place called Hell. That is the ultimate punishment for our sin. On top of that, this verse also refers to earthly deaths. There is always a death attached to sin. If you lie, then a friendship may die. If you commit adultery, then your marriage may die. If you gamble away all of your money, then your financial security may die. If you abuse drugs or alcohol, then your health and well-being may die. Death is always the consequence of sin. That has been the truth since the beginning.

I don't think I have to spend much time convincing you that you are sinful. In fact, that is probably the way in which you most see yourself. First John 1:8 says, "If we say we have no sin, we deceive ourselves, and the truth is not in us." That is not an argument I have had with anyone recently. We tend to constantly beat ourselves up over our sin. We resonate much more with Paul in Romans 7:15 when he wrote, "For I do not understand my own actions. For I do not do what I want, but I do the very thing I hate." We are constantly in a battle with our sin. All of us have said (many times) to ourselves or to God some form of, "I'll never do that again." Then, in a much shorter time than we would like to admit, we do the very thing that we said we would never do again. We get extremely angry and speak very harshly to ourselves. So, we go back to prayer, repent, and say, "I'll never do that again. This time, I'm serious." Lo and behold, we go and do that thing again. This is the struggle we all find ourselves in day after day. This is our spiritual battle. We want to live for God. We know his words and that which he asks of us. We truly want to honor him, but we keep failing.

The reason for that is because sin is a liar, and we fall for its empty assurances. Hebrews 3:13 tells us that sin is characterized by "deceitfulness." Sin always makes wonderful promises to us. It tells us that we can find joy and happiness in it. Let's be real, most sin feels good at the moment. Sex outside of marriage isn't so prevalent because it's terrible. As long as it is consensual, sex is going to feel great while it is happening. It was created by God as a gift to those who are married, as well as to promote the making of children. Sex simply for pleasure will always pale in comparison to doing it with someone that you love, trust, and to whom you have committed your life. Sex is an expression of love, not a substitute for it. Greed seems right at the time. Who doesn't want more money? So what if someone gets hurt along the way? Your job is to look out for you and your family. More money means a better and easier life, right? The problem with greed is that it will never be satisfied. You will always want more. Drunkenness is fun while it lasts, but it can quickly lead to a dependency that will wreck your life. Getting even with someone that hurt you or someone you love will surely make you feel better. Except that, after the fact, you realize it did nothing to heal the pain. Sin constantly lies to us. It tells us that the quick fix is what we need, the easy path is the way to go, and it will bring us true happiness. It fails to deliver on its promises, every single time. Don't forget that the serpent in the Garden was clever and crafty. His ways have not changed.

So, what can we do about our sin? The first thing we can do is arrive at an understanding that we are in a lifelong conflict. As I alluded to earlier, you are not the only one who has this struggle. Aside from the Savior, every person who has taken a breath has had to endure the same fight. James 4:1 refers to it as a "war within you." You can comb through the pages of the Bible and find person after person who has fought this battle. Some did better than others, but all failed one way or another. Though the times have changed, the human heart has not. As Ecclesiastes states, "There is nothing new under the sun" (1:9). That, most of all, includes the fact that all people have a flawed, sinful nature. I am not referring simply to the scoundrels and sketchy, but the heroes of scripture fit into this category, too.

Let's start with Noah. Most people know the story of him and his ark. In a land full of sin and corruption, God saw Noah as righteous (Genesis 6:9). He built the ark, filled it with the animals, and saved humanity. That is typically where people assume his story stops, but there's more. The last time that we see him, he is passed out drunk and naked. His son walked in on him and saw him this way, which brought great shame on Noah and his son (Genesis 9:20–22). This was not his ideal ending.

Then, there is Jacob. He was actually a twin and the younger brother, by a mere second or two, of Esau. Esau was the first born of Isaac and Rebekah and would have been in line to receive everything from his parents when they passed. However, Esau was tricked by his younger brother into exchanging his birthright for a bowl of stew. Jacob used manipulation to get what was not his. Even still, God blessed Jacob (Genesis 27). If you're not familiar with the rest of his story, God went on to later change Jacob's name to Israel (Genesis 32:28). He is the father of a nation that goes by the same name that still stands today.

Now, let's talk about perhaps the most important figure in Jewish history: Moses. Before he went out and talked to the burning bush, crossed the red sea, received the ten commandments, and led the Israelites through the desert, he found himself in some pretty hot water. Moses, through God's provision, was raised by the Egyptian pharaoh's daughter and received the advantages that would bring. Even though he was raised by the pharaoh's daughter, Moses knew that he was a Jew. One day, he saw an Egyptian man beating a Jewish man. He decided to step in and eventually killed the Egyptian man. Scared, he buried the body in hopes that no one would ever find out. Then, he saw two men who shared his ethnicity fighting the next day. He stepped in to try and break it up. That's when one of the men asked Moses if he would kill them too. Afraid, Moses fled from Egypt. He was correct to do so because the pharaoh did want to kill Moses for his transgression. All of that takes place in Exodus 2:11–15. Moses was a murderer, and God still used him as the major player in the rescue plan for his people.

There is also Jonah. He was a prophet called by God to go preach to the Ninevites. After trying to run away and being swallowed by a giant fish, he reluctantly went. His preaching was superbly effective, and the Ninevites repented and turned to God. Jonah wasn't happy about it, and the book bearing his name ends with him being angry and upset about what had happened. At no point in that story was Jonah's heart ever where it needed to be.

We can even move to Jesus' followers and find more people who struggled with their sin. Peter denied knowing Christ because he was more concerned for his own safety than he was for his allegiance to the Messiah (John 18:15-27). Matthew was a tax collector, which means that he worked for Rome and extorted his own people (the Jews) to gain his own wealth (Matthew 9:9). Tax collectors were the most hated people in Israeli society at that time because they were seen as traitors. Thomas doubted that Jesus had resurrected (John 20:25). Though not one of the twelve disciples, Paul made a living ravishing the early church. He presided over the murder of Stephen, the first Christian martyr (Acts 8:1). Those four men went on to change the world as preachers of the Good News of Jesus Christ, yet all of them had their struggles with sin.

I am really going to hammer this point home by sharing with you the story of Israel's greatest king: David. This is the same man that rose to the occasion and fought Goliath when no one else would. He killed the giant—armed with only a sling, a rock, and his faith (1 Samuel 17:23-50). This is the same man who had a chance to kill Saul, who had become a corrupt king, but chose not to because David believed Saul was God's rightfully appointed king (1 Samuel 24:10). This is the same David who united Israel, won battle after battle, and God called, "A man after his (God's) own heart" (1 Samuel 13:14). Seems like a pretty solid guy. Afterall, he is revered, even today, in Israel for his faithfulness and leadership. Of course, that is not the full story of David.

Let us turn to 2 Samuel 11 and look at what happened. One day, while the Jewish army was out battling the Ammonites, David decided to not do his kingly duty and go with his men into war. Sin number one. Instead, he stayed at home in his palace. He decided to look out the window when he saw a beautiful woman named Bathsheba bathing on her roof. Instead of turning away, he continued to watch her. Sin number two. Rather than leave it there, he had his people go and investigate who she was. It turns out she was a married woman. That did not stop David; he decided that he still wanted to sleep with her. Sin number three. He had his men bring her to him, and they had sex. Sin number four. As it turns out, David impregnated Bathsheba on that day. In order to cover up his debauchery, David sent for Uriah, Bathsheba's husband, who was out at war, to come home. His plan was that once Uriah was home, surely, he would sleep with his wife. David's plot was sin number five. Uriah was an upstanding man and refused to go to his house while his countrymen and the Ark of the Covenant were in battle. Instead, he slept in front of the door to King David's palace. David then decided to get Uriah drunk so that then he would lose his senses and go to his wife. Sin number six. This still did not work, and Uriah never went to be with Bathsheba. At a loss, David sent the faithful Israelite back to the front lines. Rather than face the consequences of his actions, he concocted another scheme. This time, he sent a letter with Uriah to the generals that read, "Set Uriah in the forefront of the hardest fighting, and then draw back from him, that he may be struck down, and die" (2 Samuel 11:15). This is exactly what happened, and David oversaw the murder of Bathsheba's husband to hide his own sin. Sin number seven. Once the deed was finished, David then married Bathsheba. To me, this is the most diabolical and heinous scene in all of scripture.

I recount David's story and count his sins because he is the story of us. This is the story of how quickly life can spiral out of control. We make one mistake that leads to another and another and another, and before we know it, we have found ourselves much further down the path than we would ever want to be. Look at David's original sin in 2 Samuel 11; he failed to uphold his kingly obligation of being with his army. I'm sure he had a perfectly good justification for making that choice. He certainly had no intentions or thoughts of becoming a murderer by the time that series of events played out. This is exactly how many people find themselves in a situation in which they do not want to be. You make one bad decision, and even if it doesn't seem overly terrible at the time, it gets the ball rolling.

Take those who have become addicted to drugs or alcohol. No one ever makes the conscientious decision to become an addict. It starts off by wanting to have some fun or to numb the pain that they're feeling. Then, before they ever realize it, they have become chemically dependent upon the substance. This is true for many of the habitual sins in our lives. Whether it be greed, lust, porn, gluttony, promiscuity, dishonesty, deception, materialism, selfishness, pride, etc., no one starts on the path by wanting that sin to overtake their lives. It unfortunately just takes one wrong choice for it all to spiral out of control. Before we know it, our lives have become infested with transgressions.

David went on to eventually, and somewhat reluctantly, confess his sin to God after his friend Nathan got on his case. A little aside, whenever someone that truly loves you tries to point out areas of your life in which you are struggling, please listen to them. David cried out, "I have sinned against the Lord" (2 Samuel 12:13). There is supreme truth in what he said. Yes, he also sinned against Bathsheba, Uriah, and his countrymen, but ultimately, all sin is against God.

God has designed a perfect way in which we should live our lives. Like any good parent, his rules are to help us thrive and succeed. We too often think that they are there to hold us back. Whenever we sin, we tell God that we don't think he knows what is best for us, and we're going to do things our way. This is why sin is such a big deal; it is us telling God that we are better at running our lives than he is. Spoiler alert: we are not.

The good news is that David's story did not end there either. God responded (through Nathan) to David with this statement, "The Lord also has put away your sin; you shall not die" (2 Samuel 12:13). Though there were consequences for his rebellion against God, David went on to lead Israel for around thirty more years. There were many more successes and failures along the way. His sins did not prevent God from using him. That is the truth for everyone that I have mentioned in this chapter. All of our biblical heroes, aside from Jesus, failed in one way or another. Every one of them, at some point, fell into sin. Many walked further down the wrong path than they would have ever wanted. At no point did it disqualify them from God's love.

I have already said that there are always consequences to sin, and that is true. Those tend to be earthly consequences, though. The loss of God's love is never one of those consequences. We can never take our eyes off of the fact that he is our father. Just as my dad was disappointed in my brother and me for burning down the storage building, God may be disappointed in us from time to time. Rest assured, my dad never stopped loving us for our actions, and your heavenly father will never stop loving you. That is simply not in his nature. Angelus Silesius once stated, "If God stopped thinking of me, he would cease to exist."[2] Now, that statement can easily lead to quite the theological discussion. My advice is to not go down too deep of a rabbit hole with that quote. Rather, absorb the essence of it. You are so dear to God that his love for you —yes, you—is central to who he is. It doesn't matter how far down the wrong road you have traveled; God is always going to be beckoning you to come back to him. He will always welcome his beloved child back home with open arms.

In some of his final words, David went on to say about God, "Great salvation he brings to his king, and shows steadfast love to his anointed, to David and his offspring forever" (2 Samuel 22:51). Even after all of his failures and atrocities, David knew that he was deeply loved by God. Although he didn't always live up to what God had desired for and from him, God still used David in many, many ways. That is the same for you and for me. God will still use us in more ways than we can imagine. Our usefulness is not dependent upon our goodness. It is simply dependent upon God's love for his children.

We will never be able to completely live the way in which God has designed for us. We will falter far more times than we ever should. We will regularly tell our father that we know better than him. Somewhere along the way, we will think it's a good idea to spiritually play with matches, and we'll burn down more than just a storage building. That's the battle that will wage on inside of us every day of our lives. This is a battle that we cannot actually win. We do not have the strength or might to overcome our sin. If left

2. Quoted in Manning, *Ruthless Trust*, 8.

to our own devices, we do not stand a chance. Oh friends, thanks be to God that we are not left to our own devices. God speaks the same thing to us that he spoke to David nearly three-thousand years ago, "The Lord also has put away your sin; you shall not die" (2 Samuel 12:13). Your sin has been completely wiped away. You have been forgiven, and you shall receive life everlasting. Though we cannot win the battle, God stepped in on our behalf and secured our victory. That is what we will discuss in the next chapter.

9

A Change of Clothing

SO, WE'RE SINNERS. HERE'S the thing, the previous chapter is the only chapter in this entire book where I am going to focus on that fact. Some people want writers and preachers that will pound the pulpit and keyboard with words of hellfire and brimstone. They want writers to spend a hundred and fifty pages berating the reader. Their idea of evangelism is to make others feel as lousy as they feel about themselves. That is not my aim here, nor will it ever be. Why would I focus on a problem when there is already a solution? I may get criticized for being too one-sided in my writing, but I can live with that. Afterall, Jesus did say, "I must preach the good news" (Luke 4:43). Why then has the news that the church has been preaching become so bad? Why is it that the church has turned off so many? From the outcasts to the addicts, the adulterers to the alcoholics, the broken to the belittled, the divorced to the debased, cynics to sinners, all have come to feel unwelcome inside the stained-glass adorned church walls. It seems that the only ones who feel welcomed are the self-righteous. The pews are filled with pharisees instead of the perverse. Have we forgotten what Jesus said in Mark 2:17? "Those who are well have no need of a physician, but those who are sick. I came not to call the righteous, but sinners." The church was not created for those who are perfect; it is meant to be a beacon of hope for those who are broken.

We need to shift our spiritual eyes to the good that was done for us, rather than the bad that we constantly do ourselves. Preaching Hell does not lead people to salvation. As someone who has been in youth ministry for more than a decade, I have seen this play out time and time again. Events will pop up, such as The Judgement House. They take participants, usually teenagers and younger, on a tour of Hell and tell them that's where they're heading if they do not straighten up their act. This does not lead to a changed heart but to temporary behavior modification.

I remember being at a Christian music festival in Kentucky called Ichthus when I was thirteen years old. There was a service on the final day of the event in which there was preaching and communion. I can still vividly recall what the climax of the preacher's message was, "If you died today, would you go to Heaven or Hell?" I thought to myself, "I don't know." His very next words were, "If your answer is, 'I don't know,' then you are going to Hell." This scared me, nearly to death. We then had the opportunity to talk to someone there if we wanted to go to Heaven. Naturally, that sounded much better than the alternative. If my options had been Hell or Des Moines, Iowa, then I would've given my heart to Des Moines that day. Two of my friends and I went into the tent and talked to a counselor. According to their record keeping, three souls were saved in that conversation. I am the only one still following Christ today; that has very little to do with what the preacher and counselor had to say.

My heart was not transformed in that tent. The only thing that happened was that I was scared of the idea of going to Hell. I don't disagree with the preacher's statement about what "I don't know" means. What I do disagree with is how the good news of Jesus Christ was shared at that service. The Great Commission tells us to "Go therefore and make disciples of all nations, baptizing them in the name of the Father and of the Son and of the Holy Spirit, teaching them to observe all that I have commanded you" (Matthew 28:19–20). What Jesus has commanded us to do is love

God and love others. If what we are preaching is not rooted in love, then we simply are not preaching Christ. If all that is accomplished is that people are informed that they're going to Hell, then we have sold what happened on the cross and at the tomb short. The most amazing act of love cannot be simplified to "Heaven or Hell." Jesus came to set us free from our sin. Yes, Heaven is the final result of that, but there is so much that will be missed in the here and now if the only focus is on where we will spend our eternity. There is life to be enjoyed with the Savior today— not just in the great forever.

The solution to our sin problem really is quite amazing. If you are not aware of what that solution is, then let me fill you in. If you have made it this far in the book, then you are aware that there was a man named Jesus. He was not merely a man, but he was also fully God. Jesus lived a perfect, sinless life. He went around preaching, teaching, and performing miracles, far more than what is covered in this book. The centrality of his message was that he is God, and whoever believes in him will have life with him, both now and eternally. He taught often about loving one another and being kind. He also frequently spoke against greed and self-righteousness. The religious leaders of the time hated him. His message ran counter to the privilege that they habitually abused. Despite the fact that Jesus was constantly fulfilling prophecy and doing no wrong, those wicked men decided that he needed to die. He was messing with their power (and corollary, their money), and they just couldn't stand for such things. They charged Jesus with blasphemy and tried him in a kangaroo court. He was declared guilty, even though there was no evidence to substantiate their claims. His punishment was to be beaten and then crucified; a penalty meant only for the worst of the worst. Fun fact, we get the word *excruciating* from crucifixion. In Latin, *ex* means from, and *cruci* means cross. It was so painful that the Romans, who created the practice and spoke Latin at the time, had to invent a word to describe it. Take that in for a second. There was literally not a word in their entire language that could encapsulate the pain that was felt from being nailed to a cross. At no point during all of this did Jesus object because this was precisely what he came to do.

You see, from the beginning, God made a way for sins to be forgiven. Throughout the Old Testament, the Jews sacrificed different animals to make amends for their sin. That was the system that God set in place and was practiced until the Temple was destroyed in 70 AD. Sin must have a sacrifice to gain forgiveness. God forever made provision for us when Christ was offered up as a sacrifice. The killing of animals would have continued in perpetuity if something had not been done. Christ came to this world for one reason, to offer himself up as payment for our sins. That is what happened at the cross. Christ became our forever sacrifice. Hebrews 7:27 tells us that, " . . . He did this once for all when he offered up himself." All that is asked of us is to believe that this is true.

Something spectacular happens when we put our faith in that. The fancy theological term for it is substitutionary atonement. Atonement means to make right a wrong. When Jesus died for us, he took on our sin. The first half of 2 Corinthians 5:21 says, "For our sake he (God) made him to be sin who knew no sin . . . " Jesus, because he was sinless and perfect, was able to pay our debt with his death. He was the substitute on our behalf. But wait, there's more! Not only was he given our sin, but he also gave us back something in return: his righteousness. To continue on with 2 Corinthians 5:21, " . . . So that in him we might become the righteousness of God." In exchange for our sin, we are granted Jesus' righteousness. How's that for an uneven trade? By placing our faith in Christ, we are seen as eternally *righteous* and *good* by God.

The following scene plays out in Zechariah 3. It is understandable if you are not familiar with this particular minor prophet. In this chapter of the book bearing his name, we are brought into a vision that Zechariah was having. There was the High Priest by the name of Joshua who was standing before the angel of the Lord. Sidenote, anytime in the Old Testament when you see *the* angel of the Lord, it's Jesus making an appearance prior to his birth. This is called a Christophany. If it says *an* angel of the Lord, then it is just a run-of-the-mill angel. To Joshua's right was Satan, who was there to accuse him. How I see this scene playing out is that Satan was telling Jesus every sin that Joshua has ever committed. Then, in verse 3, we are informed that the High Priest was in "filthy garments." This is symbolic of the fact that he was considered unclean because of his sin.

Have you ever been around someone who was literally filthy? I think back to when I was an elementary school student. There was one kid in particular that fit the bill. Let's call him Matt. I went to a small school in a small town, so Matt and I would often be around each other. Even though I could not totally perceive what was wrong with him, I was fully aware that something wasn't right. His clothes were always dirty, and he had an odor about him. On top of that, it was obvious that he struggled in school. Because of this, Matt was always treated poorly by the other students. I remember being in the same 6th grade social studies class as him and how kind the teacher was to him. This was not a teacher who had a reputation of being particularly nice. Even in my prepubescent mind, I recall being happy that someone was offering compassion to Matt because it was not something he regularly received. Many years later, through some strange and seemingly random happenstance, I found out what the reason was for Matt's situation. It turns out that he was raised by a single mom who greatly neglected and abused him. Eventually, he was taken away from her by the state. I can never imagine what it would be like to have a mom who did anything but care for and love me. Matt's circumstances were not the result of anything that he did, but just, unfortunately, the situation into which he was born.

We are all spiritual Matts. We are all born into a situation that is not our fault, but it affects our lives in every way. Each one of us is born into sin, and because of that, we are spiritually unclean— just like the Samaritan woman from John 4 and the blind man from John 9. We are unworthy, and there's not a thing that we can do about it ourselves. Matt didn't choose to be born into the circumstances that he was, nor did we choose to be born into sin. There was nothing that Matt did to get himself out of the position he was in, but someone eventually stepped in on his behalf and saved him. This is what God did for us through Jesus on the cross. It was the greatest act of compassion that the world has ever seen.

Let's return to the Zechariah passage. As Satan accused Joshua, Jesus spoke, "Remove the filthy garments from him" (Zechariah 3:4). Not only did Joshua have his clothing removed, but he was then dressed in clean clothes, from head to toe. Jesus then went on to say in that same verse, "Behold, I have taken your iniquity away from you, and I will clothe you with pure vestments." In this vision, Joshua was forgiven of his sin. He was dressed in pure, clean clothes to signify that he had been made righteous in the eyes of God. That is the same deal that we get when we believe that Jesus came and died for us. Joshua did not change his own clothing, but he was undressed and dressed by another. We cannot change out of our own dirty attire. We need someone to rescue us and give us new clothes. Jesus did that for us. He gives us the opportunity to have our "filthy garments" removed and to be clothed in robes of white. That is the solution to our sin problem. Jesus put on our dirty garments in exchange for us getting transfigured into his blindingly white ones. All that is asked of you is that you believe it to be true.

Most people's stories end at their death, but that was not the case for Jesus. In fact, his greatest work was about to happen. After the religious leaders thought that the supposed blasphemer had died, they wanted to make sure. In order to do this, they took a spear and drove it deep into his side (John 19:34). This elicited no reaction because Jesus had already passed and willingly accepted the consequence of our sin that we deserve. They then pulled Jesus off of the cross and put him in a tomb. This was on a Friday. On the following Sunday, the most miraculous of miracles happened.

Mary Magdalene, one of Christ's most faithful followers, went to the tomb to mourn over her lost friend, savior, and hope. As she arrived at the tomb, the stone that they had rolled in front of the entrance was gone. Although scripture does not say, she must have stuck her head in to see what was going on. To her shock, Jesus' body was gone. She then turned and ran to Peter and John, two of Jesus' closest companions, and told them what had happened.

Immediately, they sprinted to the burial site. That is when John included one of the greatest details in all of scripture, "So Peter went out with the other disciple (John), and they were going toward the tomb. Both of them were running together, but the other disciple outran Peter and reached the tomb first" (John 20:3–4). John felt that it was totally necessary to let the world know, for all of time, that he was faster than Peter. The story could have easily been told without him pointing out that his friend was slow, but it certainly does make me smile every time that I read it. For that, I am thankful. The two men went in and saw that the body was indeed gone. Not knowing what to do with this information, the two men went back to where Mary had found them. I wonder who got there first.

The grieving woman stood outside of the tomb with tears streaming down her face. The man who had cast demons out of her and saved her life was not only dead, but his body was missing. In the Jewish tradition, there were customs that needed to be performed for the dead, but this was impossible if there was no body. Suddenly, two angels appeared in front of her in the tomb and asked her why she was crying. She told them that someone must have taken Jesus' body. She then turned around and saw a man that she thought was a gardener. This man asked her the same question as the angels. Brokenhearted and confused, she asked the man if he was the one who took Jesus' body away. That gardener then said something that she was not expecting— her name. This story takes place in John 20:5–16.

It was in that exact moment that Mary knew she was talking to the Messiah who was alive again. Jesus' death and resurrection is the greatest miracle of all. I do not believe that these are two events that can be separated. They are one, three-day-long work of God. In the church, we talk far more often about the cross than we do the empty tomb, but one cannot stand on its own without the other. If Jesus would have died on the cross and that was the end of his story, then that would have meant he was simply just a man. Countless people have been killed by crucifixion, but only one came back from the dead. If the story ends at the cross, then we are not forgiven, accepted, or made to be children of God. The resurrection matters just as much as the cross. It was Jesus pronouncing triumph over sin on our behalf. When he walked out of that tomb nearly two thousand years ago, he was on a victory march. He had fought and won the battle that we have been losing since the beginning of time. Not only that, but he also invites us to join in that triumphant procession. Through substitutionary atonement, we are given that victory. He is shouting that we can have our filthy clothes removed and be dressed in dazzling white. Jesus offers us all what we have been seeking in this world. He gives us love, freedom, and compassion.

The resurrection matters because that was Jesus' most declarative statement that he is God, and all that he said is true. The only thing that is asked of us is to believe it for ourselves. To admit that we cannot win the battle, that we need a change of clothes, and that we are in need of a savior. When you do that, you will hear Jesus calling you by your name. He will throw his arms around you and welcome you home. Christ went through an unimaginable amount of pain and suffering so that we could be one with him, both here and in paradise. He did it all so that we could have a right relationship with our heavenly father. Second Corinthians 5:17 tells us that, "Therefore, if anyone is in Christ, he is a new creation. The old has passed away; behold, the new has come." We have been remade into new and perfect creations. Through faith in Christ, when God looks at us, he doesn't see any mistakes that we have made. He doesn't see any of our shortcomings. He sees neither a failure nor a sinner. Instead, he sees his precious child for whom his son gave his life. He sees us as righteous.

This may be hard to believe. Because we most often see ourselves as failures, we doubt that this can be true. This mindset comes naturally to us. If things are too good to be true, then we doubt that they can be. Perhaps the most famous case of doubting in human history is Thomas (one of the twelve disciples). This poor guy has been given the adjective of "doubting" in front of his name ever since his most famous moment, as if he's the only one to ever doubt God. After Jesus' death and resurrection, the risen Savior decided to visit his disciples. They were locked away and hiding.

That didn't stop the risen Messiah from walking into the room, though. He spent some time with them, talked to them, and gave them a mission. However, Thomas wasn't there. Later on, Thomas returned to the group, and they told him what had happened. Naturally, he didn't believe them and doubted their story. The next week, Jesus returned to the group. This time, Thomas was there. Instead of chastising or belittling Thomas, Jesus had the doubter place his finger in the nail holes in his hands and the spear wound in his side. Jesus finished by telling Thomas, "Do not disbelieve, but believe. . ." All of that story can be found in John 20:24-29.

The biggest takeaway that I get from that story is that Jesus was not angry with Thomas when he doubted. Instead, he proved to him that he was who he said he was. That is how Jesus is always going to operate in our lives. He is not out to get us when we fail to fully believe. Whether it is doubt that he will forgive you, doubt that he will be there for you, doubt that he will provide for you, doubt that he will turn your bad situation into good, doubt that he loves you, doubt that he has a plan for you that far exceeds anything that you could ask or imagine, etc. Jesus is not in the damnation business. He is in the blessing business. That does not change whenever we struggle to believe it. His goodness is not dependent upon our understanding of it. He is good regardless. It comes down to if we accept it in our lives or not.

Our friend Brennan Manning once said, when speaking at a conference, "I am now utterly convinced that on judgement day the Lord Jesus is going to ask each of us one question and only one question: Did you believe that I loved you?" That is the question each of us must ask ourselves: do I really believe that Christ came and died for me? We tend to use plurals when we talk about for whom Jesus died, but we should also look at it in the singular as well. Yes, he died for the whole world, but he also died specifically for you. You are priceless and precious to him. In John 15:13, Jesus said that he laid his life down for his "friends." That is what he considers you— a friend. Think of it this way, Jesus chose to die so that we could spend our lives and eternity in everlasting friendship with our Savior. You mean that much to him.

You mean the world to God. You are so incredibly loved by him that I cannot possibly explain it even if I were to spend my life trying to do so. His love for you and for me does not make sense. We constantly screw it up. We are always failing to do what he asks of us. Our hearts are always lusting after other things to fulfill what only the love of the Father can. None of that matters in the long run, though. We are his children. That is enough for him. He has decided that he will do whatever it takes to have a relationship with us. He sent his son into this world solely to die an excruciating death on our behalf. He does not want to see his children running around in filthy clothing. That is why Jesus did what he did. He came to make us into new, clean, righteous creations. He came to bridge the gap that our sin created. He came to lead us to the path back home. It doesn't matter where you have been or what you have done. God is not shocked by any of it. He is not afraid of your doubts. It doesn't matter how dirty you have become. No one is so far off that God's grace cannot save them. You cannot out sin God's love. The cross and resurrection are the evidence of that. How much more can he do to let you know that you are loved beyond measure?

The question for you is: do you believe that? Do you believe that it was all done for you? Do you believe that God made a way for you through Jesus? Do you believe that he will clothe you in beautiful, white garments? Do you believe that you can be made clean and a new creation? Most of all, do you believe that you are loved? Not for anything that you can do, but because he has chosen to love from now until forevermore? Here's the thing, it is all true. Yes, it runs counter to what society tells us. It goes against what the person in the mirror is constantly yelling at you. You must decide if you are willing to believe what the world tells you or what your father tells you. His children are more precious to him than anything. He loves you, here and now, exactly as you are. If you believe that, he is going to call you by name. Although, it won't be by the name your parents gave you. God will call you by the name that was given to you through the cross and Jesus' resurrection— *my beloved child.*

10

The Other Kyle Smith

As you are aware of by this point, my name is Kyle Smith. That is not a terribly unique name by any stretch of the imagination. I have always wished that my parents would have named me something far more interesting, but what is done is done. I'm sure that there are thousands of other Kyle Smiths running around in this world at this moment. In fact, I grew up with someone who had the same name as me. This created a staggering amount of confusion in school, even though he was one grade ahead of me. Outside of sharing the same moniker, we had absolutely nothing in common. We were constantly getting confused for one another. I would often be questioned about something I did, even though it was not me who did it. Many, many times in my life, I had to say, "That wasn't me. That was the other Kyle Smith." I would be amazed at how people that knew me would get us confused, even my own parents.

I came home one day after school during my freshman year of high school, and my mom said those dreaded words that sends a chill down the spine of every child, "We need to talk." Immediately, my mind began racing. I thought of everything that I had ever done wrong that she did not know about. I knew that I was going to be confronted for some wrongdoing. She asked, "Why are you failing science?" This was news to me. Admittedly, science was not one of my stronger subjects, but I thought that I was doing fine in that class. I retorted, "I'm not." "I got a letter from the school saying that you are." I knew that there must have been some mistake. I asked her if I could see the letter. After she let me look it over, I spotted the issue. "Mom, this says that I'm failing tenth grade science. I am only in ninth grade science." So, we began to try to figure out what had happened. Eventually, I surmised that they had confused me with the other Kyle Smith. She called the school and told them what happened. I received a few more of his letters. Each time, my mom would inform them of their error. Finally, they stopped sending letters to my mom's house. Of course, a few weeks later, they sent the letter to my dad's house, and I got to do that song and dance again.

Fast forward to the end of my freshman year of college. I had just completed the finals of my first year of college and was all set to head home for the summer. The morning that I was leaving to go home, I had a voicemail from my stepmom asking me where I was. This was odd because my family knew when I was coming home. I called her back and told her that I hadn't left yet. She informed me that the police had been to their house in the middle of the night looking for me. The only thought that I could muster up at that moment was, "What?" "The police came pounding on the door at four in the morning looking for you. They said that they pulled over a car, and everyone got out and ran. They were told that one of them was Kyle Smith." I took a second to gather my thoughts, laughed, and said, "That must have been the other Kyle Smith."

All throughout my life there has been another with whom I was often confused. Every time that I got accused of his actions with my parents, teachers, and friends, I wondered to myself, "Who do you think that I am?" These are the people who knew me better than anyone else, yet they believed that I would do these things that went against who I was. It was like there were two of me. I eventually started identifying myself as the "good" Kyle Smith and him as the "bad" one. I thought much too highly of myself as a teenager. Come to think of it, I still haven't outgrown that.

As Christians, we all suffer from an identity crisis in our lives. We want to be the good and faithful followers that God desires of us. We want to be the perfect little children of our heavenly father. We are so moved by his love and Christ's sacrifice that we feel we are obligated to live out our allegiance to him without blemish. We so long to hear these words spoken about us by God, "Well done, good and faithful servant" (Matthew 25:21). We want to make our dad, our Abba, proud. But we just cannot seem to be able to do so consistently. We are the living embodiment of Romans 7:19, "For I do not do the good I want, but the evil I do not want is what I keep on doing." There truly are two versions of ourselves living in each of us, the good and the bad. This is the war that is waging inside of us at all times, to do right or to do wrong. If we were to have the scales of justice placed in front of us and our good was put on one side and bad on the other, then I doubt things would tip in the way that we most desire. We have spent a lifetime failing to live up to God's desire for our lives. Because of that, we have bought into the lie that we are the "bad" version of ourselves that will periodically do something good. This, my friends, is absolutely false.

What if I told you that you are a saint? That may seem like much too lofty of a title for me to give to you, but I am not the first one to call you that. That was God. There is exactly one caveat that makes you a saint: believing in Christ. That word is used fifty-nine times throughout the New Testament (according to the English Standard Version) to refer to those who are followers of Jesus. Being a saint is not about what you do. That word has been used by the church for around two thousand years and has been given to those who were the cream of the crop. That was not its intended use. It was meant for those broken people who have embraced and accepted that God loves them, and Christ died for them. It was meant for every person who would trust that John 1:12–13 was written about them, "But to all who did receive him, who believed in his name, he gave the right to become children of God, who were born, not of blood nor of the will of the flesh nor of the will of man, but of God." We have been made saints not because of what we have done or not done, but because of what was done for us by Jesus. Though we struggle with being the "bad" version of ourselves, that is not who we are. According to God and his word, we are his children, and we are his saints. Romans 8:1 tells us that, "There is therefore now no condemnation for those who are in Christ Jesus." That evil that you do that you do not want to do does not remove the incredible designation that has been given to you. You have become a good, righteous saint. That is who you are.

I will offer up a brief caveat: this does not give us a license to go and sin freely. Just because there is no condemnation for those who believe in Christ does not mean that God condones all that we do. As I have stated before, sin will always have earthly ramifications. There will always be death attached to it, one way or another. Paul wrote about this in Romans 6:1–2, "What shall we say then? Are we to continue in sin that grace may abound? By no means! How can we who died to sin still live in it?" We are a new creation, so we should do everything in our power to avoid sin. One of the reasons that we do this is to avoid the consequences of sin. How many times must we touch a hot stove before we realize that it only brings pain? More importantly though, we avoid sin so that we can honor God and show others that we are his followers. The word the Bible uses in 2 Corinthians 5:20 is "ambassadors." We are God's representation in this world to those who do not know him. If we want the world to know who it is that we worship and believe in, then we must follow his design for our lives. Besides, his way leads to a life full of joy. It won't necessarily be an easy life, but it will be a fulfilling one. We set ourselves apart from the world by living holy lives full of love for God and love for others. We do not elude sin and do good to gain salvation, but to show our salvation.

There is something amazing that happens once we become believers in Christ. Not only does the Father call us saints, but we become filled with the presence of God. "Whoever believes in me, as the Scripture has said, 'Out of his heart will flow rivers of living water.' Now this he said about the Spirit, whom those who believed in him were to receive . . . " (John 7:38–39). Those are the words of Jesus promising to send to us the Holy Spirit. I would argue that the Holy Spirit is the least mentioned member of the trinity. If you are unfamiliar with what the trinity is, allow me to try to explain. God exists in three parts: the Father, the Son, and the Holy Spirit. They are three separate entities. However, they are all one. Confusing? I agree. The best analogy that I have for it is an egg. The egg consists of the shell, the white stuff, and the yolk. They are the three separate parts of an egg, but they all make up one egg. This, to me, is the hardest thing to explain in the Bible. It is one of those things that we must believe without fully understanding. I think the word for that is faith.

Have you ever stopped and thought about the fact that God is physically dwelling inside of you at this very moment? It truly is mind-blowing to try to wrap one's mind around it. The very same God who created the world is now living in each of us. There has been a progression of how God has lived amongst his people throughout history. It started in the desert where God led the Israelites out of Egypt as a pillar of cloud by day and pillar of fire by night (Exodus 13:21). Then, they built the Tabernacle (a big tent) for him. This was placed at the center of the Jewish camp while they were wandering from Egypt to the Promised Land and until the Temple was built. That was done during the reign of King Solomon. He had them build it in the center of Jerusalem, and it lasted about four hundred years before the Babylonians destroyed it. About seventy years after the original temple's destruction, the Jews built the second Temple. This one lasted until the Romans tore it down in 70 AD. As the pillar and in the Tabernacle and Temple, God's presence lived around his people. When Jesus was born, he became God's presence that lived amongst his people. At Pentecost, the Holy Spirit was fully given to those who believed in Jesus. God's presence was no longer merely around his people in a structure, nor with his people through his son, but moved into the hearts of his followers. You are God's modern-day temple.

You are the place in which the Holy Spirit has decided to take residence here in this world. Is that how you foremost define yourself? There are a lot of things that go into forming our identities.

Some of those may include familial identities, our careers, our favorite sports teams, the college that we went to, our accolades, the state in which we were born, our country, our achievements, our political party, etc. One of the things I was forced to learn after my marriage ended was that it would also become a part of how I am identified. My whole life, whenever I would fill out a form and be asked my marital status, I would always check "single." Now, I have to check "divorced." Sometimes in life, the world is going to force on us identities that we may or may not like. One of the chief desires of the human heart is to figure out who we are. We spend our whole lives searching for that answer. This is what God has to say about who you are in 1 Corinthians 3:16, "Do you not know that you are God's temple and that God's Spirit dwells in you?"

One of the greatest identities we have been given is that of being free. The Bible makes it clear that there are two types of people in this world, those who are slaves to sin and those who have been set free through believing in Jesus. We have been given freedom from the shackles of sin. Galatians 5:1 tells us that, "For freedom Christ has set us free; stand firm therefore, and do not submit again to a yoke of slavery." We have the power to choose that which is right and of God. We have the power to say no to sin. We have the power to tell that "other" self, the one that wants us to do that which we know that we ought not do, that he or she does not have authority over us. It is almost like the classic cartoon trope of the person who has an angel on one shoulder and the devil on the other when making a decision. One is telling you to do good, and the other is telling you the opposite. Except, this is not some made up gag used for comedic purposes. We have the presence of God directing us It is up to us if we want to listen because, ultimately, we have the freedom to say yes or no.

Obviously, we all know that we should say yes to that which we feel God is leading us to, but we are often hesitant to do so. We have so many fears and anxieties about where he is leading us. It is only through the Holy Spirit that we can be like Isaiah and say to God, "Here I am! Send me" (Isaiah 6:8). Let's look again at David when he was chosen to be king in 1 Samuel 16:1-10. God sent

Samuel, his prophet, to David's dad, Jesse, to anoint one of his sons to be king. Samuel told Jesse to line up all of his male offspring. After the prophet gave them a look over, God told him that none of them were his chosen one. Samuel then asked Jesse if he had any other sons; to which Jesse replied, "There remains yet the youngest" (1 Samuel 16:11). There was so little thought of David that his own dad didn't even bother to bring him out as a candidate. Of course, he was the one that God picked to lead Israel and be the lineage in which Jesus would be connected. David was just a boy and nowhere close to being ready to be king when God chose him. There is also Peter, who was a lowly fisherman and a nobody. Yet, he was the one about whom Jesus specifically spoke, "on this rock I will build my church" (Matthew 16:18). Was Peter prepared to be the leader of the early church at that moment? Absolutely not. In both of those cases, and many others, God chose someone to do a task far before they were prepared. The only way that they were capable of saying "yes" was because of the Holy Spirit.

You see, on our own, we cannot possibly fulfill that which we have been called to do. This is true for specific callings on people's lives and for the general call to love God and love our neighbor. Thankfully, this is where the Spirit steps in for us. Second Timothy 1:7 speaks to this, "For God gave us a spirit not of fear but of power and love and self-control." God knows that we will forever struggle in the battle to live pure and holy lives, so he stacked the cards in our favor. If we can't live up to the standards in which he desires for us, then he is going to move into our hearts and make it possible himself. We need help in order to truly love God and others. Have you ever noticed that the fruits of the Spirit are not about us but about fulfilling that call to love? "But the fruit of the Spirit is love, joy, peace, patience, kindness, goodness, faithfulness, gentleness, self-control; against such things there is no law" (Galatians 5:22–23). There are a few that pertain to us, but really, they are to help us treat others better. We are created to be beacons of God's light in this world. He has given us the Spirit to make it possible. It is up to us to tap into the endless well of God's power. It is the only way that we are going to make it in this world. For some reason, we neglect doing so and try to do it on our own.

As I stated previously, I take my students to a youth conference every year called Resurrection. One year, while singing along with the worship band, one of my students told me that he wasn't feeling well. I told him to sit down and catch his breath because I thought that he was overheating. He sat there for a few minutes and then asked one of the other leaders to help him to the restroom. As he was standing up, he fell back down into his seat. The leader and I each grabbed an arm and started to walk him out of the auditorium. As we came to the end of the aisle, he collapsed. This immediately sent me into a panic. We laid him down on the seats. When I looked in his eyes, I saw nothing; they were totally lifeless. I sprinted to the medical personnel and told them what had happened. Eventually, he came to and had the most frightened look on his face. He asked me, "What happened?" I told him, and then the EMTs began to ask him questions. Finally, we found out what the culprit was. He hadn't drunk any water that day. Combine that with the overheating, and you have a recipe for dehydration. After he drank a couple bottles of water, he was good to go and back to normal.

I tell you that story as an analogy for what happens when we do not tap into the Holy Spirit in order to do what it is that God has called us to do. That student knew he needed to drink water, but he chose not to. Of course, he had no thought that he was harming himself. That is often the same mindset that we have. We neglect to do what we need to do to keep ourselves spiritually healthy. We ignore going to the eternal spring that is in us for a drink. We think the Holy Spirit is in a glass box that reads, "Break in case of emergency." That's not the case, though. If we try to live Godly lives on our own power, then we will eventually collapse under the weight of the burden. We need the Holy Spirit to be active in us in order to be women and men of God.

The big question is how do we allow the Holy Spirit to be in the driver's seat of our lives? We first do that by acknowledging that we have an identity crisis. We always have the battle inside of us between the good and the bad, the holy and the heathen, the saint and the sinner. Denying this truth does nothing for us. We need to search deep down inside ourselves and find those areas in which we demand that we be in control. No matter how long we follow God, there will always be places in our lives where we think we should be the one pulling all the strings. To give way to the Spirit's leading, we must let go of ourselves. This is what Jesus was referring to in Luke 9:23 when he said, "If anyone would come after me, let him deny himself and take up his cross daily and follow me." We must be able to accept that we are not the ones who should sit on the throne of our own lives. Then, we need to pray and ask the Spirit to lead us. After that, it is simply about doing everything we can to love those around us. This may sound simplistic, but it will prove to be impossible for us. We so dearly want to operate in autonomy despite knowing that it leads nowhere good. If we are willing to lay aside our perceived power and ask the Holy Spirit to lead, he will gladly do so.

We have the power of the living God dwelling inside of us. This is given to all of God's beloved children. That is a power far greater than anything in this world. That power gives us the freedom to choose God each and every day. When we wake up each morning, we must decide if we are going to take control of our lives or allow the Spirit to guide us. It is the struggle of two dancers who each want to be lead. The Holy Spirit will not force his way but is always ready to act at a moment's notice. We get to choose which identity we want to embrace. Each of us must choose which way to go. You can either chase what the world offers and fall prey to the façade that it can truly satisfy your soul, or you can tap into the presence of the one who created that soul. You are God's temple on this planet. The Holy of Holies resides within you. Because of this, you have been made holy, righteous, and clean.

In Joshua 24:15, the namesake of the book cries out, "Choose this day whom you will serve!" Will you serve the world that tells you constantly that you are not good enough, that you will never amount to anything, and that you are a failure? Or will you choose to serve your heavenly father who loves you so much that he couldn't stand to be separated from you, so now his spirit dwells in you? How do you wish to identify yourself? Is it by all the temporal and meaningless ways that society has pushed on you or is it by something infinitely greater and eternal?

I am Kyle Smith, the son of Joe and Kathi Smith, Youth Pastor, Miami Dolphins fan, graduate of Marshall University, brother, uncle, author, and divorcee. All of that is, as Paul said, "rubbish" (Philippians 3:8). Here is the identity that truly matters. I am Kyle Smith, deeply loved and cherished by my heavenly father, someone whom Christ chose to die for, God's holy temple, saint, and child of God. Those are the titles that will last throughout all of time. I am not unique in any of those. They are all offered to you. They are all freely given to you. They were all purchased for you by the death and resurrection of Christ Jesus our Lord. God loves you, and Christ died for you. All that truly matters is who you are and whose you are. Everything this world offers you will fade away. What your father offers you will stand the test of time. Do you believe that? Will you believe that? Do not let anyone, including yourself, ever tell you that you are anything less than what your Abba says you are. He will always call his beloved child by the name that he loves to call you the most—*mine*.

Afterword

THROUGHOUT THIS BOOK, YOU have read about how God loves you. That has been the singular focus. I believe that to be a blanket statement. No one resides outside the love of our heavenly father. I hope that I have not presented you with any new information. I wish that everyone who wanders this earth knew that their Abba has a deep, deep affection for them. Sadly, that is not the case. Many people are presented with the wrong image of who God is. Some have never heard about him, some think he is distant and not caring, some understand him as simply punitive, some think that he exists as a genie who grants their wishes, and some think that he doesn't exist at all. They have been sold a false idea of who God really is and have never heard that, "God is love" (1 John 4:8). The point of this book is simply to let everyone who reads it know that they are cherished by their creator. God loves you, Christ died for you, and the Holy Spirit lives in all of those who believe that to be true. Ultimately, that is all I really wanted to say. That sentence conveys all the truth I ever aspired to share. Everything else was just filler.

If this was new information or old information heard in a new way, then what are you to do with it? I'll let a story from the life of Jesus speak to that.

> On the way to Jerusalem, he was passing along between Samaria and Galilee. And as he entered a village, he was met by ten lepers, who stood at a distance and lifted up their voices, saying, "Jesus, Master, have mercy on us."

When he saw them, he said to them, "Go and show yourselves to the priests." And as they went, they were cleansed. Then one of them, when he saw that he was healed, turned back, praising God with a loud voice; and he fell on his face at Jesus' feet, giving him thanks. Now he was a Samaritan. Then Jesus answered, "Were not ten cleansed? Where are the nine? Was no one found to return and give praise to God except this foreigner?" And he said to him, "Rise and go your way; your faith has made you well" (Luke 17:11–19).

Leprosy is a disease that basically rots away your flesh. It is easily curable now but was a terminal condition back in biblical times. It was also believed to be highly contagious, although it was not. Because of this, those who contracted the infection were forced to move into leper colonies away from society. Just imagine what the living conditions of a small inhabitation filled with people whose skin was rotting away must have been like. They were not allowed to come close to, let alone touch, anyone. In fact, whenever they would come into town for any reason, they would have to yell, "unclean," so that the other people would know to stay away. Quite a life, eh? They were outcasts who were all alone, just waiting for death to take hold.

In the scripture passage above, Jesus was greeted by a group of lepers when he was spotted going into a village. His reputation had preceded him. Any sane person at that time would have run in the opposite direction— not Jesus. He immediately sent them to the religious leaders. The law required anyone who was free of their leprosy to go to a priest to be given the seal of approval. They all went as directed. As they walked, they were healed of their mutual ailment. From that point on, we have no idea what happened to the nine of them. Having received what they desired and with a new lease on life, they may have gone to their homes to be with loved ones for the first time in who knows how long. However, there was one that returned. He came back to thank Jesus for what he had done.

This is to be our response for all that is laid out in this book: thankfulness. We are to be thankful for the work of God, Jesus, and the Holy Spirit in our lives. We can never repay them for the love that has been greatly lavished on us. We can try and should try, but we will always come up far short. The best that we can do is to live our lives out of thanksgiving for what we have been given. This is done by praising the Father, the Son, and the Spirit. We need to make it a regular practice of ours to fall down at the feet of Jesus and pour out our admiration for him. We need to regularly confess to the Holy Spirit that we cannot do it without him and give him control. We need to regularly crawl up into the lap of our good and grace-filled father and spend time with him. Along with that, we should tell others, in word and deed, about this great love, too. That is all that we need to do. Stop trying to work yourself to death to prove something to God. He doesn't want your accomplishments or resumé; he simply wants you, just as you are.

Friends, you are far more loved than you can ever dare to dream about. You are eternally adored by the God who made you. You are so precious to him that he sent his son to die for you and is now willing to dwell in your heart. I can assure you that this is no exaggeration as to how your father feels about you. Quite simply, it is impossible to overstate his feelings for you. You are his beloved child, bought for a price. You are the apple of his eye. You are that for which his heart beats. All that is asked of you is your acceptance of that truth. He has done all that he can to show it to you. Let me state one more time what 1 John 3:1 says in the Holman Christian Standard Version, "Look at how great a love the Father has given us that we should be called God's children. And we are!"

And we are!

Bibliography

Hamilton, Adam. *Revival: Faith as Wesley Lived it*. Nashville: Abingdon, 2014. 139

Luther, Martin, and Theodore G. Tappert. *Luther: Letters of Spiritual Counsel*. Vancouver: Regent College Pub, 2003. 86–87

Merriam-Webster's Collegiate Dictionary. 11th ed. Springfield, MA: Merriam-Webster, 2003. Also available at http://www.merriam-webster.com/.

Manning, Brennan. *Abba's Child: The Cry of the Heart for Intimate Belonging*. Colorado Springs, Colo: NavPress, 2002. 60

Manning, Brennan. *Ruthless Trust: The Ragamuffin's Path to God*. San Francisco: HarperOne, an imprint of Harper Collins, 2002. 8

Manning, Brennan. *The Furious Longing of God*. Colorado Springs, CO: David C. Cook, 2009. 43–44

Pascal, Blaise. *Pensees*. Paris: Éditions du Seuil, 1978. 75

Pollock, John. *Amazing Grace: John Newton's Story*. London: Hodder and Stoughton, 1981. 182